"The world was peopled
with wonders."

The origin of Wildsam comes from above, a
line of prose in the novel *East of Eden,* written by
John Steinbeck. Six words hinting at a broad and
interwoven idea. One of curiosity, connection, joy. And
the belief that stories have the power to unearth the
mysteries of a place—for anyone. The book in
your hands is rooted in such things.

We explored Boston at a unique moment in the city's long history, a time when we couldn't haunt archives or linger on barstools in our usual way. Deep thanks go to the proud Bostonians, present and past, who guided us to the city's soul: David Modigliani, Elle Simone Scott, April Gabriel of Boston General Store, Dean Russell, Nina Berg and Matthew Boyes-Watson of Flagg Street Studio, Mark Peterson, Lee Glandorf at Tracksmith, Jonathan Belton at Topdrawer, Marina Aslanidou and Kimberley Lowthers at the Whitney, Dawn Griffin at the Isabella Stewart Gardner Museum and others. Extra gratitude to Dart Adams for a wander through the streets and alleys of the South End/Lower Roxbury.

WILDSAM FIELD GUIDES™

Copyright © 2021

Published in the United States by Wildsam Field Guides, Austin, Texas.

ISBN 978-1-4671-9939-1

Illustrations by Julia Emiliani

To find more field guides, please visit www.wildsam.com

# CONTENTS

*Discover the people and places
that tell the story of Boston*

# WELCOME

———

**IN EARLY DAYS,** Boston often became an island. A sliver of dirt, the Neck, connected the Puritan colony to the mainland, just yards wide in spots and prone to flood. When waters rose, the Neck vanished. The settlers floated off the shore of the continent, a true ocean city.

Then as now, though, Bostonians seldom rested. They knocked down hills, filled in bays and created new land—South End, Back Bay, South Boston. Roxbury went from farm village on the Neck's far end to an engine of the city's own history. And so the cozy, brick-lined cityscape that feels ancient by our standards is really radically new. To look at today's map is to see a different city, with only ghostly outlines of the old.

It just happens to be the same place. Boston remains singular, its people loyal and distinct. Different, proud of it, islanders in their hearts. Boston is the rare American city started not only due to trade or convenient geography, but because its founders were on a mission. They wanted a City upon a Hill, ennobled by shared purpose. Solidarity, we might call it now. Bostonians, of course, fell short on this vision many times. The city's origin collides with Massachusett, Wampanoag and other Indigenous histories; enslaved Africans and famine-scattered Irish did not exactly *choose* Boston. After 400 years, Boston presents a social puzzle as complicated as any. But to paraphrase local boy Ted Kennedy, the dream never died.

You can walk forever on the streets of Boston. It feels like at every crooked corner, you encounter the story of a breakthrough or signal moment. The characters now might speak Haitian Creole or Cape Verdean Portuguese, but the plotlines connect to the city's original aim to make the world anew. Or step off the street, into the Museum of Fine Art's halls. Portraits by John Singleton Copley bring the city's big Revolutionary names right into the room—Paul Revere, Sam Adams, Mercy Warren. It's 1760 or so, and these folks already glimmer with self-possession and a sense of destiny. Two centuries later, Allan Rohan Crite's paintings of Black life in Roxbury hum with human spirit and community. And then you meet Polly Thayer, a 1920s painter of a local school. Her self portrait, *The Algerian Tunic*, brings us face-to-face with a woman wearing a mod haircut and a knowing gaze. Her style is a little bit traditional, but her ambitions are all about tomorrow. Behold, a Bostonian. —The Editors

# ESSENTIALS

FRIDAY
Pastry at Flour in Beacon Hill
Newbury Street shopping swing
Celtics game at TD Garden

.......................................

SATURDAY
Emerald Necklace walk
Woodbury Poetry Room, Harvard
Dinner at Pammy's
Late pint at the Phoenix Landing

.......................................

SUNDAY
BEC croissant, iced coffee
    at Dunkin'
Gardner Museum browse
Fried-oyster bun, Eventide
    Oyster Co.

MEMENTOS

Seagull sweatshirt, *Sault New England*, $58
Taza Chocolate Classics Collection, $28
Customized sneakers, *Converse Flagship*, $115

RECORD COLLECTION

| | |
|---|---|
| Boston | *Boston* |
| New Edition | *Heart Break* |
| Dropkick Murphys | *Do or Die* |
| Ed O.G & Da Bulldogs | *Life of a Kid in the Ghetto* |
| Joan Baez | *Joan Baez* |
| Nancia | *Heir to the Throne* |
| Pixies | *Surfer Rosa* |
| Big Thief | *Capacity* |
| New Kids on the Block | *Hangin' Tough* |
| Aerosmith | *Toys in the Attic* |
| Gang Starr | *Step in the Arena* |
| Modern Lovers | *The Modern Lovers* |
| The Cars | *Shake It Up* |
| Palehound | *A Place I'll Always Go* |

# ESSENTIALS

LODGING

Whitney Hotel
*170 Charles St*
Chic, warm, creative base for Beacon Hill.

......................

907 Main
*907 Main St Cambridge*
Good drinks at the Dial, zesty design.

......................

Verb Hotel
*1271 Boylston St*
Mod rocker, a fly ball from Fenway. Deep vinyl stack.

......................

Fairmont Copley Plaza
*138 St James Ave*
Grand hotel in Back Bay, founded 1912.

The Charles
*1 Bennett St Cambridge*
Harvard visit HQ. Big Regatta vibes.

......................

Studio Allston
*1234 Soldiers Field Road*
Vibrant student-quarter art retreat.

......................

Boston Harbor Hotel
*70 Rowes Wharf*
Palatial. For when your ship comes in.

......................

Lenox Hotel
*61 Exeter St*
Classy/playful in a Boston way. Great local connections.

Eliot Hotel
*370 Commonwealth Avenue*
Home to Uni, a dressy izakaya.

......................

Fort Hill Inn
*3 Centre Pl*
Full apartments in a Roxbury town house.

......................

The Colonnade
*120 Huntington Avenue*
Crisp rooms, rooftop pool.

......................

XV Beacon
*15 Beacon St*
Moody mainstay in the lantern-lit power center.

---

WELLNESS

*Trillfit*
A community-oriented, woman-owned operation blasts inclusive energy, with hip-hop workouts and nonprofit links. *1484 Tremont St*

......................................................................................

*Peter Welch's Gym*
Old-school Southie fight guy [first bout, age 9] now runs all-around fitness classes infused with pugilistic realness. *371 Dorchester Ave*

......................................................................................

*Root + Sky Wellness*
A Winthrop, MA native with deep training recruits top practitioners for acupuncture, yoga and reiki. *1140 Saratoga St*

*Museum of Fine Arts, Boston*
Americas collection, 3,000 years deep, is just one strength.

.........................

*Isabella Stewart Gardner Museum*
A dreamlike art palace built on one woman's legacy.

.........................

*MassArt*
Experimental creative flair across genres.

.........................

*List Visual Arts Center*
MIT's arts hub is heady, as it should be. Multimedia ambition.

*Museum of African American History*
Art, artifacts trace Black Bostonians across 400 years.

.........................

*Gropius House*
The architect's home in Lincoln offers a stellar Bauhaus collection.

.........................

*JFK Presidential Library and Museum*
Full Camelot immersion.

.........................

*Harvard Art Museums*
Trinity of distinct museums lets bright minds roam, ancient worlds to now.

*ICA Boston*
A globally significant center for modernism and contemporary art.

.........................

*Warren Anatomical Museum*
Throwback medical wonders. Venerable skulls and hips.

.........................

*Mary Baker Eddy Library*
Check out the three-story Mapparium.

.........................

*USS Constitution Museum*
Climb aboard Old Ironsides, or play the website video game of sailor life.

---

PERFORMANCES

Symphony Hall
*Among the best acoustics anywhere*

.........................

The Sinclair
*Indie sets in Cambridge's heart*

.........................

Wang Theatre
*1925 room for big-ticket shows*

.........................

The Dance Complex
*Crossroads of pro shows and classes*

Cambridge Elks Lodge
*Punk scene's "Hardcore Stadium"*

.........................

Opera House
*High culture, architectural gem*

.........................

Boston Center for the Arts
*Ambitious, future-facing shows*

.........................

Wally's Cafe Jazz Club
*Scene linchpin since 1947*

# ESSENTIALS

## BOOKSTORES

**Brattle Book Shop**
*9 West St*
Enchanted new-and-used shrine since 1825.
.......................

**Frugal Bookstore**
*57 Warren St*
Nubian Square bastion of Black lit.
.......................

**Porter Square Books**
*25 White St, Cambridge*
Smart seller squad, plus its own non-profit literacy foundation.

**Brookline Booksmith**
*279 Harvard St Brookline*
Finger-on-pulse picks and events.
.......................

**Trident Booksellers**
*338 Newbury St*
Beloved for vast selection and cafe.
.......................

**Raven Used Books**
*23 Church St, Cambridge*
Erudite finds [philosophy, history] for Harvard Square.

## COFEEE

**George Howell**
*505 Washington St*
.......................

**Broadsheet**
*100 Kirkland St*
.......................

**Caffé Vittoria**
*290-296 Hanover St*
.......................

**Gracenote**
*108 Lincoln St*
.......................

**Cicada**
*106 Prospect St Cambridge*

---

## HISTORIC HOMES

### Paul Revere House
*19 North Square*
The original midnight rider's crib—a rare American city house of 1600s vintage—hosts smart historical discussions, re-enactments.
.......................................................

### Nichols House Museum
*55 Mount Vernon St*
Beacon Hill town house, maybe designed by Charles Bulfinch, America's first pro architect. Significant arts and crafts collection.
.......................................................

### Cooper-Frost-Austin House
*21 Linnaean St, Cambridge*
Cambridge's oldest domicile shows off "lean-to" architecture.
.......................................................

### Harvard Lampoon Building
*44 Bow St, Cambridge*
"Home" of the famous/infamous undergrad humor mag. Fake-Flemish castle. Hidden chambers. *Crimson* rivals sometimes pilfer ibis statue.

# ISSUES

| | |
|---|---|
| Traffic & Transport | Boston's roads ranked as the country's most congested in 2018 and 2019. The "T," the city's subway, has the second-worst derailment record among major U.S. systems. Failed bids to host the Olympics and Amazon's HQ2, with mobility woes cited in both cases, underscore the urgency to find fixes. **EXPERT:** *Chris Dempsey, Transportation for Massachusetts* |
| Housing | One recent study found Boston the nation's third most "intensely gentrified" city. East Boston [a.k.a. "Eastie"], home to a majority-Hispanic/Latino population, is the latest zone of rising rent, but community leaders aim for equity. **EXPERT:** *Gloribell Mota, Neighbors United for a Better East Boston* |
| Hunger | Massachusetts' hunger rate increased 59 percent since 2018, with 1 in 5 children living in food-insecure households. Pandemic efforts distributed food to laid-off restaurant workers, while local nonprofits like Lovin' Spoonfuls serve Bostonians facing food issues. **EXPERT:** *Tracy Chang, Project Restore Us* |
| Historic Buildings | In a city founded in 1630, building anything new often means getting rid of something really old. Neighborhood sentiment, affordability concerns, antiquarian passion and monied interests make a volatile mix. **EXPERT:** *Greg Galer, Boston Preservation Alliance* |

STATISTICS

.482 ...................... Ted Williams' career on-base percentage [MLB record]
> 430 ............................... Est. number of Massachusetts biotech firms, 2019
$350,000...................................Price of a single Beacon Hill parking spot, 2018
5.3M ................... Barrels of beer produced by Samuel Adams brewery, 2019
$36B..................... Est. value of today's Boston that was underwater in 1630
34 ............................... Islands and peninsulas in Boston Harbor Islands Park
2.3M........................Metric tons of cargo entering Boston Harbor annually
130,000 ........................ Est. number of undergrads and grad students, 2018
$9,500 ................Donations to busking icon Keytar Bear after 2017 assault

# NEIGHBORHOODS

### JAMAICA PLAIN

Founded by Puritan farmers. Now Boston's crunchiest corner.

**LOCAL:** *Tres Gatos, Brassica Kitchen, Papercuts Bookshop*

.............................................

### FENWAY-KENMORE

Vintage ballpark meets very shiny new development.

**LOCAL:** *Sweet Cheeks, Hojoko*

.............................................

### ROXBURY

Bustling hub for Black culture.

**LOCAL:** *Hibernian Hall, Suya Joint, Fasika Cafe*

.............................................

### CAMBRIDGE

Bracing mix of Harvard, MIT and a global-village populace.

**LOCAL:** *Cambridge Deli & Grill, Silk Road Uyghur Cuisine*

.............................................

### SOUTH BOSTON

Southie. Irish of old, beloved for brick patina, water views.

**LOCAL:** *Fat Baby, Castle Island, American Provisions*

.............................................

### NORTH END

Trattorias and caffes in a maze.

**LOCAL:** *Giacomo's, Bova's Bakery, Sulmona Meat Market*

### CHARLESTOWN

A classic tangle of homes and history in the Bunker Hill monument's shadow.

**LOCAL:** *Brewer's Fork, Monument Restaurant & Tavern*

.............................................

### SOUTH END

Culture in medley, with stories from all corners and a bright, artsy present-day identity.

**LOCAL:** *South End Buttery, Petit Robert Bistro, Gallery Kayafas*

.............................................

### BEACON HILL

Regal Boston at its cobbled best. Narrow alleys, hidden gardens, John Kerry sightings.

**LOCAL:** *Beacon Hill Pub, 21st Amendment, Toscano*

.............................................

### BACK BAY

Once saltwater, now a jigsaw of brownstone blocks and primo retail flaneur territory.

**LOCAL:** *Uni, Bukowski Tavern, Asta, Alan Bilzerian*

.............................................

### BROOKLINE

Traditional Jewish crossroads. Also JFK's birthplace.

**LOCAL:** *Allium Market, Larz Anderson Park, Zaftigs*

SOMERVILLE ○

CHARLESTOWN ○

CAMBRIDGE ○

EAST BOSTON ○

NORTH END ○

BECAON HILL ○

○ BACK BAY

CHINATOWN ○

FENWAY-KENMORE ○

SOUTH BOSTON ○

SOUTH END ○

BROOKLINE ○

○ LOWER ROXBURY

○ ROXBURY

○ JAMAICA PLAIN

○ WEST ROXBURY

# BESTS

*A curated list of city favorites—classic and
new—from bars and restaurants to shops and experiences,
plus a handful of surefire experts*

# FOOD & DRINK

*For our Seafood and Irish Bars maps,*
*see pages 72 and 73.*

### BISTRO
Juliet
*263 Washington St*
*Somerville*
Bringing all-day joy
with sunny Mediter-
rean verve, wild-
card Sunday supper
menus, profit-share
for workers.
...........................

### ITALIAN BAKERY
Mike's Pastry
*300 Hanover St*
*North End*
Amid an unending
North End *dolci*
debate, this is the
venerable champ.
Take the cannoli.
...........................

### TASTING MENU
Tasting Counter
*14 Tyler St*
*Somerville*
Inspiring big-ticket
night: an all-in pass
for intense seasonal,
regional bites.

### NEW ENGLAND
Loyal Nine
*660 Cambridge St*
*Cambridge*
The region's farm
and sea connections
get a spotlight. Will
serve no stinging
nettle or sea urchin
before its time.
...........................

### TAPAS
Toro
*1704 Washington St*
*South End*
Ken Oringer's
hymn to vermut and
small plates warms
the soul. Ham-
burguesa sliders.
...........................

### SOUTHERN
Darryl's Corner
*604 Columbus Ave*
*South End*
Embassy of gumbo,
jambalaya and Texas
toast, with live jazz
at center stage.

### DUMPLINGS
Mei Mei
*506 Park Dr*
*Fenway*
Irene Li, acclaimed
champion of
progressive industry
thinking, also wields
a mean cheddar-
scallion packet.
...........................

### PIZZA
Regina Pizzeria
*11 1/2 Thacher St*
*North End*
Wood oven, brick-
lined space, deep
queues of loyalists.
The definitive
Bostonian slice.
...........................

### OYSTERS
Neptune Oyster
*63 Salem St*
*North End*
Steadfast source
of New England
bivalves, lobster rolls
and convivial scenes.

**WEST AFRICAN**

Obosá

146 Belgrade Ave
Roslindale

Nigerian dishes,
plated with artistic
precision.

.........................

**BÁNH MÌ**

Bánh Mì Ơi

1759 Centre St
West Roxbury

Eleven sandwiches.
The baguettes alone
keep fans obsessed.

.........................

**ENOTECA**

Fox & the Knife

28 W Broadway
South Boston

Italo-classics, cacio
e pepe to vongole,
given sharp twists by
lauded chef Karen
Akunowicz.

.........................

**RAMEN**

Ganko Ittetsu

318 Harvard St
Brookline

Sapporo wok meth-
ods amp flavors.

.........................

**BAGELS**

Kupel's Bakery

421 Harvard St
Brookline

Kosher bakery with
a devoted following
and stacked lineup.

**DATE NIGHT**

Pammy's

928 Massachusetts
Ave, Cambridge

Kick back in a
beloved trattoria's
leather banquettes.

.........................

**DIM SUM**

Hei La Moon

88 Beach St
Chinatown

Sprawling [but low-
key] favorite for char
siu bao, cart delights.

.........................

**ROAST BEEF SANDO**

Billy's Roast Beef &
Seafood

1291 Main St
Wakefield

North Shore folks
will argue about
this. Just make the
pilgrimage.

.........................

**TURKISH BAKERY**

Sofra

1 Belmont St
Cambridge

Chocolate-hazelnut
baklava? Wicked.

.........................

**FILIPINO**

Tanám

1 Bow Market Way
Somerville

Kamayan feasts as
entryways to deeper
cultural stories.

**COCKTAILS**

Drink

348 Congress St
South Boston

Southie gal Barbara
Lynch's place. Tell
'em what you like.

.........................

**DIVE BAR**

Silhouette Lounge

200 Brighton Ave
Allston

All cash. Free pop-
corn. Twinkle lights.
Fuzzy memories.

.........................

**OLD HAUNT**

Warren Tavern

2 Pleasant St
Charlestown

That Colonial
thing, going strong
since 1780. Wash-
ington, Bunker Hill
and Revere lore.

.........................

**DISTILLERY**

Bully Boy

44 Cedric St
Roxbury

Crack the bottled
Old Fashioned.

.........................

**BREWERY**

Lamplighter

284 Broadway
Cambridge

Bright, shiny takes
on European styles.
Try Stupid Seagulls.

# SHOPPING

### ART BOOKS

Ars Libri
*500 Harrison Ave*
*South End*

Supplier to scholars, with stacks of curated collections, documents and rarities reaching deep into history.

.......................

### GIFTS

Olives & Grace
*623 Tremont St*
*South End*

Sharply chosen picks for the most deserving on your list, rooted in community connections and spirit.

.......................

### COFFEE & TEA

Polcari's Coffee
*105 Salem St*
*North End*

Glorious, aromatic jumble of beans and goods. Since 1932.

### MAKERS

Black Market
*1136 Washington St*
*Roxbury*

A pop-up rallying point for Black artisans and entrepreneurs, pushing equitable development in the area.

.......................

### VINYL

Cheapo Records
*538 Massachusetts*
*Ave, Cambridge*

One of those impeccable old-school spots. Bins and bins of every genre and a staff marinated in expertise.

.......................

### ITALIAN GROCERY

Monica's Mercato
*130 Salem St*
*North End*

Do it the North End way with a deli and fresh-pasta stop.

### HOME

Boston
General Store
*Brookline and Dedham locations*

Outfit yourself. Quality scissors. Fine toothbrushes. Cocktail shakers and sewing kits.

.......................

### COMICS

Newbury Comics
*384 Newbury St*
*Back Bay*

A pop cultural nerve center, featuring exclusive special editions from top publishers. Rare records, manga too.

.......................

### WINE SHOP

The Urban Grape
*303 Columbus Ave*
*Back Bay*

The place to get turned on to new bottles by smart folk.

## WORK AND TRAVEL
**Topdrawer**
*5 Brattle St*
*Cambridge*
Stylish goods for nomads. Imported pens, Polaroids, Boston-designed bags and eyeglasses.
.........................

## VINTAGE
**High Energy Vintage**
*429 Somerville Ave*
*Somerville*
Go grab the amazing '70s floral print before anyone else.
.........................

## WOMENSWEAR
**Ouimillie**
*126 Charles St*
*Beacon Hill*
Fresh styles with the right slice of avant-garde edge.
.........................

## PLANTS
**Niche**
*619 Tremont St*
*South End*
Transplanting vibrant tropicalia to New England. Cacti!
.........................

## SKIN CARE
**Tao's**
*35 Harrison Ave*
*Chinatown*
Dizzying global bath/body goods.

## NAUTICAL NEEDS
**Westerbeke**
*400 Border St*
*East Boston*
Century-old supplier of maritime gear. Twine loft weaves Fenway's nets.
.........................

## SNEAKERS, ETC.
**Bodega**
*6 Clearway St*
*Back Bay*
Artfully disguised sneakerhead, gear-brand gold mine.
.........................

## SPICES
**Curio Spice Co.**
*2265 Massachusetts Ave, Cambridge*
Flavors and aromas from the farthest horizon.
.........................

## STATIONERY
**Tiny Turns Paperie**
*1 Bow Market Way*
*Somerville*
A chipper and crafty touch for modern correspondence.
.........................

## HIGH FASHION
**VRSNL**
*18 Newbury St*
*Back Bay*
Streetwise takes on famed global brands and designers.

## MICROSHOPS
**Popportunity**
*Central Square*
*Cambridge*
Bootstrapping small-scale retailers united, from hair care to honey.
.........................

## HABERDASHERY
**Salmagundi**
*765 Centre St*
*Jamaica Plain*
Lids ahoy. Donegal tweed cap or elegant old-time straw.
.........................

## CHEESE
**Curds & Co.**
*288 Washington St*
*Brookline*
Abundant artisan selection, classes and cheese-keeping tips.
.........................

## LEATHER
**deWolfe Leather Goods**
*250 Newbury St*
*Back Bay*
Boston-crafted bags and accessories.
.........................

## IRISH GROCERY
**Marino's Market**
*1906 Centre St*
*West Roxbury*
Teas, breads, Tayto Crisps, Batchelors curried beans.

# ACTION

*For our maps of Charles River adventures and Boston learning, see pages 66 amd 67. For Museums, see page 9.*

### RUNNING CULTURE
Tracksmith
*285 Newbury St*
*tracksmith.com*
Neo-classic gear capturing Boston's peerless sporting heritage, plus group runs from the Back Bay Trackhouse.
..........................

### RECORD LABEL
Union Sound
*unionsound*
*.bandcamp.com*
Crowdfunded champion of local beats and hip-hop culture, with a Somerville retail shop. Colored vinyl galore.
..........................

### DANCE CLUB
Middlesex Lounge
*315 Massachusetts Ave, Cambridge*
Underground DJs with the touch. Always turnt up.

### ART STOP
National Center of Afro-American Artists
*300 Walnut Ave Roxbury*
Rich exhibits delve from ancient Nubia to bracing modern expression.
..........................

### SEA CHANTEYS
Boston Song Sessions
*bostonsongsessions.org*
Clearinghouse of pub singalongs in various corners. The Somerville Armory nights welcome all ye hearties.
..........................

### NATIONAL FESTIVAL
Cape Verde Independence Day
*City Hall Plaza*
Because July 4 marks more than one country's birth.

### SOCIAL CLUB
Society in Dedham for Apprehending Horse Thieves
*Ask around*
More partying and whimsy than equine enforcement. Michael Dukakis, member #5835.
..........................

### ROAD RACE
Boston Athletic Association 5K
*baa.org*
The marathon's organizing body launched this kickoff for the big race weekend in 2009. Unicorn medals.
..........................

### PARK BOATING
Jamaica Pond
*courageoussailing.org*
Rent craft for excursions on JP's beloved Emerald Necklace gem.

BIKE RIDES

Community Bike Supply
*facebook.com/ communitybikeboston*
Routes and rentals, with inclusive ethos.

..........................

FOLK MUSIC

Passim
*47 Palmer St Cambridge*
Heir to legendary Club 47, Joan Baez's training ground.

..........................

COMEDY TROUPE

Emerson Comedy Workshop
*emerson.edu*
Co-founded by Denis Leary. Allegedly, Jay Leno didn't make the cut.

..........................

IRISH MUSIC

The Druid
*druidpub.com Cambridge*
Hoist a pint high for weekend *seisiúns* of fiddle and accordion.

..........................

TREES

Arnold Arboretum
*@arnold-arboretum*
Extraordinary global grove. Visiting coyotes add some wild spice.

SOCCER FANDOM

The Rebellion
*Section 143 Gillette Stadium*
Scarf up and sing for the New England Revolution.

..........................

KARAOKE

Midway Cafe
*@themidwaycafejp Jamaica Plain*
Queer-centric Thursday sessions get just a bit cray.

..........................

SURFING

Ocean House
*@oceanhousesurf Swampscott*
Monitoring the NE swells from the North Shore. Rentals and lessons.

..........................

HISTORY TRIP

Salem Witch Museum
*@salemwitchmuseum*
Incisive but entertaining treatment of 1692's dark times.

..........................

ART PARTY

MFA Late Nites
*@mfaboston*
Performances and revelry, plus exhibition wanders, running till 2 a.m.

FISH

New England Aquarium
*neaq.org*
Stunning tanks, deep environmental expertise.

..........................

SPEAKER SERIES

Lowell Institute
*lowellinstitute.org*
Diverse and erudite but for the people, putting smart folk onstage since 1836.

..........................

IRISH SPORTS

Gaelic Athletic Association
*gaaboston.com*
Full-tilt battle in Gaelic football and hurling [the one with the stick].

..........................

ART HOUSE CINEMA

Coolidge Corner Theatre
*coolidge.org Brookline*
Nonprofit ark of cinematic culture.

..........................

BIRD-WATCHING

Mount Auburn Cemetery
*Cambridge*
A rich avian retreat. Olive-sided flycatcher discovered here, 1830.

# EXPERTISE

### CULTURE BEAT
Jeneé Osterheldt
*bostonglobe.com*
A writer on the rise trains her acute lens on the arts and society, telling many stories of Black Bostonian life.

.........................

### HISTORIC GEOGRAPHY
Garrett Dash Nelson
*@bplmaps*
Archive and data work to peel back the layers on New England and Boston's landscape.

.........................

### TAILOR
William Browne & Sons
617-436-9786
Masterful, quick repairs and alterations. Skills generations in the making. Locally revered.

### FOOD START-UPS
Melissa Castro
*laconexion.co*
Aiding diverse new restaurants via the CommonWealth Kitchen incubator and her La Conexión consultancy.

.........................

### CURATION
Erica Hirshler
*mfa.org*
The MFA's American painting ace expounds on individual masters and behind-the-scenes art market politics.

.........................

### CLEAN BEAUTY
Tara Foley
*follain.com*
A blogger's eye on beauty product ingredients spawned a fast-growing brand: soaps, scrubs and serums.

### SAXOPHONE
Tia Fuller
*tiafuller.com*
One of Berklee's many resident geniuses, she's played alongside Bey and powered Pixar characters.

.........................

### PHILOSOPHY
Michael Sandel
*justiceharvard.org*
What's the right thing to do? His course on "Justice" might be the most popular Harvard class of all time.

.........................

### TATTOOS
Brilliance Tattoo
*@brilliancetattoo*
A select squad of artists working at peak craft and creative levels. Bookings can be tough but worth a sharp lookout.

UNDERGROUND

Mass Cult 617

*masscult617.com*

A giant online archive gathering show flyers, old mags, ticket stubs and ephemera, R&B to punk rock.

..........................

VACCINES

Stéphane Bancel

*modernatx.com*

French-born CEO threaded COVID's many minefields.

..........................

HORTICULTURE

Erika Rumbley

*gardnermuseum.org*

Remaking the Gardner Museum's iconic plantings.

..........................

ITALIAN LESSONS

Benedetta Rossi Marangoni

*nempacboston.org*

Bologna native and multilinguist, with lessons in the North End and elsewhere.

..........................

ROBOTS

MIT Robotics Team

*roboteam.mit.edu*

Student-led campaign seeks RoboCup glory.

CREATIVE WRITING

Eve Bridburg

*grubstreet.org*

Founder of the inclusive and hard-working center for writing classes.

..........................

SUBATOMIC PARTICLES

Lee Roberts

*bu.edu/physics*

Key co-founder of recent breakthrough muon experiments.

..........................

BASKETBALL

Jackie MacMullan

*espn.com*

Standby analyst and *Around the Horn* talker, versed in pros and college ball.

..........................

OLDE THINGS

Boston Furniture Archive

*bfa.winterthur.org*

Mesmerizing online cache of craft heri-tage. Such chairs!

..........................

DOUGHNUTS

Blackbird Doughnuts

*@blackbirddoughnuts*

High-flying indie challenger to Dunkin's rule. Con-sult the FAQ for freshness tips.

FLOWERS

Forêt

*@foretdesignstudio*

Sometimes stark, sometimes lush, Erin Heath's ar-rangements have a poetic urgency.

..........................

ACTIVISM

Ibram X. Kendi

*@ibramxk*

Anti-racist bestsell-ing author aims to revive Boston's abolitionist publish-ing past with *The Emancipator*.

..........................

DEVELOPMENT

Flagg Street Studio

*flaggstreetstudio.com*

Smart, scrappy urban design and civic efforts, pop-ups to soccer tourneys.

..........................

SHOE REPAIR

Jimmy's

617-868-8838

A Cambridge go-to since 1953, now on its third generation.

..........................

LITERARY MAP

Infinite Atlas

*infiniteatlas.com*

Find every location in David Foster Wallace's *Infinite Jest*.

*Excerpts have been edited for clarity and concision.*

ALMANAC

A deep dive into the cultural heritage of
Boston through news clippings, journal entries, speeches,
timelines and other historical ephemera

# BOSTON BREAKTHROUGHS

1629......Royal charter loophole gives Boston broad autonomy

1630......Colonists swap disease-ridden Charlestown for Shawmut Peninsula

1635......Boston Latin School founded, nation's oldest public school

1636......Harvard College chartered by colony, not the Crown

1640.....Boston merchants, fishermen conquer Spanish salt-cod market

.....Continent's first English-language printing press. Psalms are a hit.

1652......Colony issues its own coins, exerting control in New England

1689.....Locals successfully revolt against Crown-declared Dominion of NE

1721......Cotton Mather and Zabdiel Boylston begin smallpox inoculations

1764.....First "committee of correspondence" opposes British policy

1779......John Adams writes MA constitution, world's oldest still in force

1813......Francis Cabot Lowell imports U.K. loom technology

1831......William Lloyd Garrison launches abolitionist paper *The Liberator*

1845......Southworth & Hawes: landmark photo studio, sexy daguerrotypes

1846.....First public surgery with anesthetic in the Ether Dome

1850.....National Woman's Rights Convention in Worcester

1863......54th Massachusetts Infantry mobilizes: famed Black regiment

1865......First classes at Massachusetts Institute of Technology

1876.....Alexander Graham Bell places first phone call in Exeter Place lab

1878.....First U.S. bicycle race held in Beacon Park

1896.....Harriet Hemenway, Minna Hall found MA Audubon

1897.....Tremont Street subway opens, America's first

.....First run of Boston Marathon, now world's oldest yearly 26.2-miler

1901......Gillette introduces safety razor, using MIT sheet-steel know-how

1904......Sturtevant brothers develop automatic transmission

1914......Technicolor launched, putting black-and-white footage on notice

1936......Institute of Contemporary Art founded. Intros many big names.

1941.....Navy Yard builds, overhauls destroyers at breakneck pace

1951......Lowell Institute launches WGBH, public radio pioneer

1961......MIT hacker club starts work on *Spacewar!*, first true video game

1964......Amar Bose launches audio gear company

1971......Cambridge consultant sends first email

1994.....World Wide Web Consortium sets the rules of browsing

2004....Harvard undergrads Zuckerberg, Saverin launch thefacebook.com

2020......Boston labs of Pfizer and Moderna work on coronavirus vaccines

# HARVARD FIGHT SONGS

*Lyrics of the Crimson's many age-old anthems
often disparage "Eli," a.k.a. Yale.*

GRIDIRON KING [*ca.* 1908]

Then hit the line for Harvard,
For Harvard wins today!
We will show the sons of Eli
That the Crimson still holds sway.
Sweep down the field again,
Victory or die!
And we'll give the grand
    old cheer boys,
When the Harvard team goes by.

ONWARD CRIMSON [*ca.* 1906]

Onward Crimson, staunch defenders
Of the emblem we hold dear,
Marching dauntless through the
    gauntlets
While the Elis quake with fear!
Stay the course now, mighty Crimson,
For the glory and the pride!
Undefeated, foes retreated,
Harvard's vict'ry sanctified.

---

## MARIA W. STEWART

*Speech to the New England Anti-Slavery Society,* 1832

Methinks I heard a spiritual interrogation—"Who shall go forward, and take off the reproach that is cast upon the people of color? Shall it be a woman?" And my heart made this reply—"If it is thy will, be it even so, Lord Jesus!" I have heard much respecting the horrors of slavery; but may Heaven forbid that the generality of my color throughout these United States should experience any more of its horrors than to be a servant of servants, or hewers of wood and drawers of water! Tell us no more of southern slavery; for with few exceptions, although I may be very erroneous in my opinion, yet I consider our condition but little better than that. Yet, after all, methinks there are no chains so galling as the chains of ignorance—no fetters so binding as those that bind the soul, and exclude it from the vast field of useful and scientific knowledge. O, had I received the advantages of early education, my ideas would, ere now, have expanded far and wide; but, alas! I possess nothing but moral capability—no teachings but the teachings of the Holy spirit.

> *Maria W. Stewart was a domestic servant, prominent among
> Boston's free community of color. Her speeches and manifestoes stand as
> milestones for women and Black Americans.*

## THE WATERFRONT

*Henry David Thoreau,* 1865

I see a great many barrels and fig-drums—piles of wood for umbrella-sticks—blocks of granite and ice—great heaps of goods, and the means of packing and conveying them,—much wrapping-paper and twine—many crates and hogsheads and trucks—and that is Boston. The more barrels, the more Boston. The museums and scientific societies and libraries are accidental. They gather around the sands to save carting. The wharf-rats and customhouse officers, and broken-down poets, seeking a fortune amid the barrels. Their better or worse lyceums, and preachings, and doctorings, these, too, are accidental, and the mall of commons are always small potatoes. When I go to Boston, I naturally go straight through the city [taking the Market in my way], and down to the end of Long Wharf, and look off, for I have no cousins in the back alleys—and there I see a great many countrymen in their shirt-sleeves from Maine, and Pennsylvania, and all along shore and in shore, and some foreigners beside, loading and unloading and steering their teams about, as at a country fair.

## THE ACCENT

It's the bane of Oscar winners, the regional seasoning for some of the country's most famous political speeches. Other regions have their drawls, twangs and big Minnesotan vowels, but the Boston accent reigns as America's most distinctive urban accent. Its signature sound is an absence: Bostonians drop their *r*'s in many contexts, as in the famed phrase "pahk the cah in Hahvahd yahd." For decades, observers associated this non-rhotic quirk with Boston's English affinities: The upper-class Brahmins of the 19th century were imitating British elites, the thinking went. But more-recent linguistic analysis sheds doubt on that origin tale. In 2012's seminal *Speaking American: A History of English in the United States*, Richard Bailey finds that early Bostonians dropped their *r*'s before fashionable Londoners started doing likewise and that Yankee speech originated as a rebellion, not imitation. [Other researchers still think East Anglian settlers brought the practice with them.] Whichever trip across the Atlantic sunk the *r*, the consonant's cancellation persists in Boston today, from City Hall to barstools in Southie, where "cheeahs" accompany the clinking of glasses. As many actors have learned, it's best not to imitate, only appreciate.

# CINEMATIC TOUR

**GOOD WILL HUNTING 1997** A genius janitor splits from Southie, with visits to Cambridge classrooms and a Charlestown therapist along the way. Matt Damon and Robin Williams in golden roles.

.....................................................................

**THE DEPARTED 2006** Enough Scorsese-style double-crossing in South Boston to make a seasoned pedestrian's head spin.

.....................................................................

**THE TOWN 2010** Cambridge-reared Ben Affleck trains a lens on the country's bank robbery capital, Charlestown.

.....................................................................

**BLACK MASS 2015** Irish mob king Whitey Bulger's violent rule of South Boston, in focus. Johnny Depp, menacing and made-up.

.....................................................................

**TED 2012** A talking teddy bear blabs and bounces around the South End.

.....................................................................

**GONE BABY GONE 2007** Ben's little bro Casey scours Boston for a Dorchester girl's kidnapper in an adaptation of a Dennis Lehane novel.

.....................................................................

**SPOTLIGHT 2015** Intrepid *Globe* journalists unearth a Catholic Church scandal from messy desks on Morrissey Boulevard.

.....................................................................

**MYSTIC RIVER 2003** A mobster's daughter's death roils fictional East Buckingham along the real Mystic River. Lehane again.

.....................................................................

**THE THOMAS CROWN AFFAIR 1968** The Financial District, Beacon Hill, Cambridge ... where doesn't handsome heister Steve McQueen take us?

.....................................................................

**CELTIC PRIDE 1996** Early Apatow, vintage Wayans [Damon], Akroyd and Stern. Fandom follies get two Garden creatures in a pickle.

.....................................................................

**FEVER PITCH 2005** Friendly Fenway gets in the middle of a Jimmy Fallon/Drew Barrymore love quest fit for a historic comeback.

.....................................................................

**THE FRIENDS OF EDDIE COYLE 1973** Classic '70s noir hard case. City Hall, urban scenes and intrigue in communities around Boston.

*Lucy Stone*

*Malcolm X*

*Julia Ward Howe*

*Elaine Noble*

*Charles Remond*

*John Boyle O'Reilly*

# REFORMERS AND RADICALS OF NOTE

**WILLIAM LLOYD GARRISON** Editor/publisher of *The Liberator*, the key anti-slavery newspaper, from 1831 to the Civil War.

.........................................................................................

**MALCOLM X** Teen turning points here: "I didn't know the world contained as many Negroes as I saw thronging downtown Roxbury at night, especially on Saturdays."

.........................................................................................

**ELAINE NOBLE** America's first open LGBTQ state legislator, elected 1974.

.........................................................................................

**JOHN BOYLE O'REILLY** Stalwart Irish activist. He escaped an Australian penal colony to became a poet, editor of Boston's *Pilot*.

.........................................................................................

**JULIA WARD HOWE** Wrote 1862 banger "Battle Hymn of the Republic."

.........................................................................................

**JAMES PLEASANT BREEDEN** Episcopal minister in Roxbury, Freedom Rider and an organizer of 1963 Boston civil rights push.

.........................................................................................

**ANNA LOPIZZO** Martyred in 1912's epic strike by Lawrence textile workers, largely Italian, demanding fair wages and hours.

.........................................................................................

**MEL LYMAN** Folkie '60s jug-band player became divisive leader of Fort Hill commune and the wild underground paper *Avatar*.

.........................................................................................

**LUCY STONE** Born 1818 of OG Puritan stock, fought for abolition and equality. First Massachusetts woman in college.

.........................................................................................

**HOWARD ZINN** Longtime Boston University prof put *People's History of the United States* on every lefty bookshelf.

.........................................................................................

**JOHN P. COBURN** Wealthy Black clothier. His upper-crust Beacon Hill gambling house doubled as Underground Railroad stop.

.........................................................................................

**MARTHA & LUCY BALL** Feminist sisters founded a West End school for Black students in 1833.

.........................................................................................

**CHARLES REMOND** Anti-slavery lecturer, activist, Civil War recruiter.

## THE GREAT MOLASSES FLOOD

*A calamity of many names—Boston Molasses Disaster, Great Boston Molasses Flood—this sticky situation occurred on January 15, 1919, as a storage tank containing 2.3 million gallons of molasses exploded, flooding the North End. Even now, residents claim you can still smell the syrupy sweetness on hot summer days.*

*Boston Evening Globe,* January 15, 1919
"15 KILLED, 150 INJURED IN NORTH END EXPLOSION"
"Molasses Tank Blows Up, Causing Widespread Damage to Property"

............................................................................................................

*The Boston Post,* January 16, 1919
"HUGE MOLASSES TANK EXPLODES IN NORTH END; 11
DEAD, 50 HURT"
"Giant Wave of 2,300,000 Gallons of Molasses, 50 Feet High, Sweeps
Everything Before It—
100 Men, Women and Children Caught in Sticky Stream"
"No Escape From Gigantic Wave of Fluid"

............................................................................................................

*The Boston Daily Globe,* January 16, 1919
"Death and Devastation In Wake of North End Disaster"
"Buildings Demolished, Sticky Mass Floods Streets—Loss $500,000"
"MARTIN CLOUGHERTY AWOKE IN A SEA OF
STICKY MOLASSES"

*See* Dark Tide: The Great Boston Molasses Flood of 1919
*by Boston historian Stephen Puleo.*

## E. E. CUMMINGS

*Prolific poet, accomplished painter and son of a Harvard professor, Edward Estlin Cummings was born and raised in Cambridge, attended Harvard and even joined the faculty. However, he rebelled against the town's academic elite. Below, an excerpt from a letter to his sister, Elizabeth, 1922.*

NOTHING IS SO DIFFICULT AS TO BE ALIVE!!!!!! which is the ONLY THING WHICH YOU CANNOT LEARN ever, from anyone, anywhere: it must come out of you; and it never can, until you have KNOCKED DOWN AND CARRIED OUT all the teachable swill of Cambridge etc.

## CHEERS

Thursday nights, we were all Bostonian, 275 times at least. We walked down the brick-lined steps, took a seat by Cliff and Norm. Sexy Sam [or Diane] poured us a cold mug. Across a 1980s generation, a sitcom greeted, initially, by humble ratings mixed gruff throwback charm with brainy wordplay—a Boston cocktail if ever there was one. The NBC stalwart lined its polished bar with an ensemble strength that TV is not likely to deliver again, from Ted Danson and Shelley Long locked in screwball combat to Kelsey Grammer's Frasier, slowly blossoming into a franchise of his own. And Woody! And Coach! And Carla! *Cheers* played a cultural role now almost forgotten, uniting so many of us around its hearth. When last call came in '93, scores of millions watched, listening to the barroom floor creak one last time, nodding along as Sam Malone said, "Boy, I tell ya, I'm the luckiest son of a bitch on earth."

### GOOD FRIDAY EXPERIMENT

*On Good Friday in 1962, a Harvard University divinity student named Walter Pahnke conducted an experiment in collaboration with the hallucinogen researchers Timothy Leary and Richard Alpert [later known as Ram Dass]. A group of students attended services at Boston University's Marsh Chapel under the influence of psilocybin. [A control group received a placebo.] One memory:*

"For me, the climax of the service came during a solo that was sung by a soprano whose voice [as it came to me through the prism of psilocybin] I can only describe as angelic. What she sang was no more than a simple hymn, but it entered my soul so deeply that its opening and closing verses have stayed with me ever since. *My times are in Thy hands, my God, I wish them there; My life, my friends, my soul, I leave entirely in Thy care.... My times are in Thy hands, I'll always trust in Thee; And after death at Thy right hand I shall forever be.* In broad daylight those lines are not at all remarkable, but in the context of the experiment they said everything."

—Huston Smith, *Cleansing the Doors of Perception: The Religious Significance of Entheogenic Plants and Chemicals*

# POETS OF NOTE

**MERCY OTIS WARREN**
Pro-Revolution poet, satirist, historian. Combative friend to John Adams.

**PHILLIS WHEATLEY**
America's first published Black poet, celebrated even while enslaved.

**ANNE BRADSTREET**
Puritan born in England, 1612. "The Tenth Muse, Lately Sprung Up in America."

**ANNE SEXTON**
Fierce, confessional midcentury verse matches a gnarled life story.

**ROBERT FROST**
Associated with rural New England, but lived three years on Beacon Hill.

**ANDREA COHEN**
Oft-published current powerhouse, runs acclaimed Blacksmith House readings.

**ELIZABETH BISHOP**
Exacting, meticulous. Not prolific. Reputation soared after 1979 death.

**ROBERT LOWELL**
Scion of Boston aristocrats. Poems dig deep into self, background.

*A starting point for exploration:* **GROLIER POETRY BOOK SHOP,**
*6 Plympton Street, Cambridge.*

# BOSTON CREAM PIE

*Though we may never know the precise origins of this confounding confection, one thing is certain: You'll find damn good renditions around town.*

| | |
|---|---|
| BIRTHPLACE: | Omni Parker House [alleged] |
| TYPE OF DESSERT: | Cake [contrary to its moniker] |
| COMPONENTS: | Pastry, custard, chocolate glaze |
| INCARNATIONS: | Whole cake, slice of cake, mini-cake, doughnut |
| WHERE TO FIND: | Omni Parker House [the mothership], Legal Sea Foods, Union Square Donuts, Flour Bakery, Dunkin', Veggie Galaxy, Mike's Pastry |

## HARVARD MISCHIEF

*Among Harvard's array of social societies, the now-defunct Med. Fac.
[a.k.a. the Medical Faculty Society] once tormented officialdom.
The New York Times explains "outrages," February 24, 1901.*

Harvard's mysterious society, commonly known as the "Med. Fac.," has been brought into prominence again this year by the perpetration of four daring acts of vandalism. The last of these, the blowing up of the old college pump, occurred on Thursday, and to-day the question which has puzzled Harvard men for the last 40 years is again on every lip—Who are the "Med. Fac.s?" This mysterious society is said to date back to the civil war, when a number of outrages, remarkable for their daring and ingenuity, were perpetrated. Each year has seen a repetition of them. At one time it was the painting of Fogg Museum, at another it was the disfiguring of the venerable John Harvard in the college yard. In each case the offenders escaped. The four offenses attributed to the "Med Facs" which have been committed this year are the explosion of a bomb in Sanders Theatre, the daring display of earthenware from the flag pole on the Cambridge Commons, the painting of the college motto, "Veritas" on the shield on Gray's Hall, and the blowing up of the old college pump on Thursday night. The old pump is dear to the heart of every college man. It has been a landmark since its erection at the beginning of the century, and those who planned its destruction must have known what a storm of indignation they would arouse.

---

## NATIONAL DAY OF MOURNING

Since 1970, the Indigenous peoples of New England have gathered at Cole's Hill in Plymouth on the third Thursday in November for a day of spiritual connection, as well as protest of the Thanksgiving holiday. The inaugural National Day of Mourning occurred when Wamsutta James, a Wampanoag man, declined to speak at the 350th anniversary celebration of the pilgrims' arrival to Plymouth. A plaque erected in honor of the Native-led United American Indians of New England organization reads: "Participants in National Day of Mourning honor Native ancestors and the struggles of Native peoples to survive today." A bus leaves from Jamaica Plain to shuttle Boston-based participants to the event, which starts at "12 noon SHARP" and is typically followed by a potluck social.

## THE BIG DIG

*The rerouting of I-93 through central Boston [1991 to 2006] became an odyssey of expense and traffic. In 2006, falling tunnel ceiling panels crushed a car, killing a passenger. Letter to the editor,* The Boston Globe, *July 15:*

A thought crossed my mind as I looked at the diagram of a cross section showing how the failed bolts were installed in the tunnel ceiling. I did not need to draw upon an introductory course in mechanical engineering kinematics—no, just experience hanging pictures into sheet rock. Clearly the patronage-job geniuses and their engineers, who are now scurrying to deflect blame, lacked such rudimentary insights. May I offer a simple solution? Redrill the bolt holes at, say, a 25-degree angle off vertical. Intuition, without drawing the vector force diagrams, should glow into the engineers' heads that the bolts could now only pull out if the whole ceiling fell. —*John C. Kotelly, Class of 1960, Massachusetts Institute of Technology, Arlington*

## ALLSTON CHRISTMAS

Among other qualities, Boston is the country's biggest college town. Students make up about one-fifth of the population, and landlords plan accordingly. It seems that all the city's apartment leases start on September 1, which makes the last days of August a hectic time of move-outs and pack-ups citywide. Enterprising Bostonians can visit any of the city's undergrad bastions and find an impressive array of household items strewn across lawns and sidewalks: kitchenware, couches, pool tables. In Allston, an affordable enclave outside the city's core, this free curbside shopping bears the cheerful name Allston Christmas. Tips on scoring big abound, but "Wash before you wear" might be the most important principle.

*Campus life pervades Boston's streets and culture. Every February, the* BEANPOT HOCKEY TOURNAMENT *sees teams from Boston University, Boston College, Northeastern and Harvard do battle.*

# THE GARDNER MUSEUM HEIST

The Boston Globe, *March 19, 1990*

In what was described as the biggest art theft since the 1911 robbery of the "Mona Lisa," two men posing as police officers gained entry to the Isabella Stewart Gardner Museum early yesterday, restrained two security guards and left with an estimated $200 million worth of art, police said. The works stolen included paintings by Jan Vermeer, Rembrandt and Edgar Degas, museum officials said. In a daring, middle-of-the-night robbery, police said, the two men knocked on a side door of the world-famous Gardner in Boston's Fenway section at about 1:15 a.m. and told the security guards there was a disturbance in the area, and were allowed to enter. Police and FBI officials said the men then overcame the guards, tied them with tape and spent about two hours in the museum, stealing 12 art objects. Acting curator Karen Haas said the $200 million estimate is conservative and the worth of the stolen works may be "hundreds of millions of dollars." … Thomas Hughes, the FBI agent in charge of the investigation, said he could not reveal details about the robbery, including how the security system, including alarms and cameras, was foiled. "We will be looking at what system was in place, how it operated, if it was bypassed and how it had been bypassed," Hughes said. He also said that while investigators believe there were two thieves involved, "there might well be more."

> *In 2009,* ARTnews *reported: "There have been no demands for ransom. None of the works has been recovered, even though the museum offers a $5 million reward and says that it 'ensures complete confidentiality' for information leading to their return. And despite thousands of tips … none of the authorities knows for sure where the works are or who stole them."*

PODCAST
*Last Seen*, 10-parter from the *Globe* and WBUR, gets deep on suspects.

BOOK
*The Gardner Heist* by Ulrich Boser offers a gritty play-by-play of the wee hours.

STREAMING DOC
*This Is a Robbery* is a binge-worthy retelling by locals the Barnicle Brothers.

# HOUSES OF WORSHIP

**FIRST CHURCH** Like it says, founded 1630 by original colonists. Key to Congregationalist [member-run] tradition that shaped New England.

.........................................................................

**CATHEDRAL OF THE HOLY CROSS** Catholic power center, deeply historic and cosmopolitan, but in the *Spotlight* of 'oos abuse scandal.

.........................................................................

**OLD SOUTH CHURCH** First Church dissenters split off in 1669. Member Samuel Adams signaled Tea Party kickoff from the tower.

.........................................................................

**UNION CHURCH** Progressive, multicultural Methodists tracing roots to Black faith gatherings in the 1790s.

.........................................................................

**OLD NORTH CHURCH** Diverse Episcopal congregation dating to 1720s. Famed beacon for Paul Revere.

.........................................................................

**FIRST CHURCH OF CHRIST, SCIENTIST** "Mother church" of the Christian Science movement, launched by Mary Baker Eddy in 1875.

.........................................................................

**ISLAMIC SOCIETY OF BOSTON CULTURAL CENTER** Roxbury-based, largest mosque in New England. Noted for interfaith efforts.

.........................................................................

**CHURCH OF THE IMMACULATE CONCEPTION** No longer active, but Italianate example of prolific Catholic architect Patrick Keely's work.

.........................................................................

**TEMPLE OHABEI SHALOM** Bastion of Brookline since 1842, Greater Boston's oldest synagogue.

.........................................................................

**OLD WEST CHURCH** 1760s minister Jonathan Mayhew stirred up trouble, boosting Unitarian movement and blasting the Crown.

.........................................................................

**TREMONT TEMPLE** Baptist landmark, successor to 19th-century abolitionist and arts-world lecture hub.

.........................................................................

**KING'S CHAPEL** Began in 1686 as Church of England outpost in Puritan New England. Claims to have the oldest pulpit in America.

.........................................................................

**BASILICA OF OUR LADY OF PERPETUAL HELP** Shrine of the Catholic Redemptorist order, associated with miracle healings.

# BOSTONIAN BOOKSHELF

**HOW I WENT OUT TO SERVICE**
*by Louisa May Alcott*
The *Little Women* author gets sassy about a dead-end job in Dedham.

**BLACK MASS**
*by Dick Lehr and Gerard O'Neill*
Reporters' two-fisted, real-life mob tale: Whitey Bulger's pact with the feds.

**THE BELL JAR**
*by Sylvia Plath*
Meteoric poet's only novel, a fraught whirl between NYC and Boston.

**MEMOIR OF JAMES JACKSON**
*by Susan Paul*
The first biography of a Black American tells a 6-year-old boy's story.

**THE BOSTONIANS**
*by Henry James*
Right-wing boy seeks liberal girl. Sharp, funny 19th-century portrait. Could be now.

**COMMON GROUND**
*by J. Anthony Lukas*
Pulitzer-winning New Journalism landmark uses '70s busing crisis to reveal city history.

**INFINITE JEST**
*by David Foster Wallace*
Postmodernist epic of addiction and tennis in weird future Boston. Hot take: It's good.

**CHAIN OF CHANGE**
*by Mel King*
A 1981 analysis of three decades of Black Bostonian history, still riveting and useful.

**THE BOSTON GIRL**
*by Anita Diamant*
A zoomed-in novel about century-back Jewish immigrant life.

**A DRINK BEFORE THE WAR**
*by Dennis Lehane*
Big-name Dorchester crime writer's deepest cut, a soulful and grimy PI tale.

**ANOTHER BULLSHIT NIGHT IN SUCK CITY**
*by Nick Flynn*
Nuts, bolts, warts and everything: an autobiographical street-life elegy.

**ON BEAUTY**
*by Zadie Smith*
A wild card from across the pond, exploring intellectual and family ferment in academic Boston.

## COMET NOTES

*Cotton Mather, age 14, scrawled notes in the back pages of an astronomical treatise.*

April 21, 1677. The Comet did rise NE by N abt. Two in the morning. And about three it was 10 degrees 15 minutes from the Bright Foot of Andromeda and 35 degrees from Capella. So the Longitude was 10 degrees off Taurus and Latitude 18 degrees N. April 23. It rose abt. a quarter past two, and distant from Capella 30 degrees 30 minutes. And from the Bright side of Perseus 17 degrees 45 minutes. So the Longitude was 15 degrees 8 minutes. Latitude 17 degrees N. Mr. Flampsses at Greenwich, observed it the same day at 28 minutes past two, and found the Longitude 14 degrees 46 minutes. Taurus and Latitude 17 degrees 4 minutes N.

*Cotton and his father, Increase, were Puritan Boston's intellectual leaders in the 1600s and early 1700s, encouraging science and public health, building the great library of their time. Cotton's role in the Salem witch trials, among other issues, makes his legacy a matter of ongoing debate. Notes above are in the collection of the American Antiquarian Society, in Worcester.*

## JOHN F. KENNEDY

*Address of the president-elect to the General Court of the Commonwealth of Massachusetts, January 9, 1961*

During the last sixty days, I have been at the task of constructing an administration. It has been a long and deliberate process. Some have counseled greater speed. Others have counseled more expedient tests. But I have been guided by the standard John Winthrop set before his shipmates on the flagship *Arbella* 331 years ago, as they, too, faced the task of building a new government on a perilous frontier. "We must always consider," he said, "that we shall be as a city upon a hill— the eyes of all people are upon us." Today the eyes of all people are truly upon us … Courage. Judgement. Integrity. Dedication. These are the historic qualities of the Bay Colony and the Bay State—the qualities which this state has consistently sent to this chamber on Beacon Hill here in Boston and to Capitol Hill back in Washington.

# THE BOSTON MASSACRE

*On March 5, 1770, a Boston mob confronted British soldiers on King Street.*
*The troops opened fire, killing five. A number of soldiers later stood trial,*
*defended by 35-year-old attorney John Adams. Excerpts*
*from Adams' notes of testimony:*

**JAMES CRAWFORD:** Went home to Bull's Wharf at dark about 6 o'clock, met numbers of people going down toward the Town House with sticks. At Calf's Corner, I saw about a dozen with sticks; in Quaker Lane and Green's Lane, met many going towards King Street. They had very great sticks, pretty large cudgels, not common walking canes.

**THOMAS KNIGHT:** At his own Door, eight or ten passed with sticks or clubs and one of them said, "Damn their Bloods. Let us go and attack the main guard first." The Bell were ringing.

**J. BAILEY:** The boys hove Pieces of Ice at sentry as big as your fist, hard and large enough to hurt a Man. Montgomery was knocked down, and his Musket fell out of his Hand, by a club or stick of wood by one of the Inhabitants, and as soon as he got up he fired.

**ARCHIBALD J. BREWER:** Saw no more abuse than was common, Met Dr. Young with a sword. Dr. said every Man to his own Home, perhaps some use may be made of this circumstance. There was a general alarm—every Body had a Right and it was very prudent, to arm themselves for their defense.

**MR. PALMS:** Montgomery slipped in pushing the third time at him and fell. In probability he killed Attucks, and continued the same mischievous spirit in pushing.

**MARSHALL:** The moon was to the north. Saw a party come out of the main guard door. Damn them, we are seven! By Jesus let them come. Boisterous language.

**BART KNEELAND:** One pointed his Bayonet at his Breast. Mr. Appleton and little Master's story and the manner of his telling it must have struck deep into your Mind. When Struck by a soldier, he tenderly asked him, "Soldier spare my life." The soldier said, "No damn you we'll kill you all."

---

*Adams secured acquittal for most defendants, but the incident primed revolutionary passions.* CRISPUS ATTUCKS, *a victim likely of mixed African and Indigenous heritage, remains a cultural touchstone, as in the 2008 lyric by hip-hop artist Nas: "Crispus Attucks | First blasted."*

♫

# BERKLEE COLLEGE OF MUSIC

*The esteemed music school's six-year graduation rate hovers near
65 percent, and the dropout list is as impressive as the alumni roster.
A sampling of artists who attended but never finished.*

John Mayer
Justin Timberlake
Quincy Jones
Donald Fagen [Steely Dan]
Melissa Etheridge
Brad Whitford [Aerosmith]
Annie Clark [a.k.a. St. Vincent]
Steve Vai

Adrianne Lenker [Big Thief]
Natalie Maines
Aimee Mann
Kevin March [Guided by Voices]
Paula Cole
Diana Krall
Ed Roland [Collective Soul]
Gillian Welch

## MAKE WAY FOR DUCKLINGS

*The General Laws of Massachusetts
[As amended Jan. 1, 2003]*

PART I ADMINISTRATION OF THE GOVERNMENT

TITLE I: JURISDICTION AND EMBLEMS OF THE
COMMONWEALTH

CHAPTER 2: ARMS, GREAT SEAL AND OTHER EMBLEMS
OF THE COMMONWEALTH

Section 49. The book "Make Way for Ducklings" by Robert McCloskey
shall be the official children's book of the commonwealth.

*The bill to enshrine McCloskey's tale of a Public Garden flock
was proposed by a third-grade class from Canton, MA. As the Boston
Globe noted on the book's 1941 publication, "it tells the story—
mostly in pictures—of Mr. and Mrs. Mallard who came to
Boston to hatch their ducklings."*

# RALPH WALDO EMERSON

*From "The American Scholar"*
Cambridge, 1837

We have listened too long to the courtly muses of Europe. The spirit of the American freeman is already suspected to be timid, imitative, tame. Public and private avarice make the air we breathe thick and fat. The scholar is decent, indolent, complaisant. See already the tragic consequence. The mind of this country, taught to aim at low objects, eats upon itself. There is no work for any one but the decorous and the complaisant. Young men of the fairest promise, who begin life upon our shores, inflated by the mountain winds, shined upon by all the stars of God, find the earth below not in unison with these, but are hindered from action by the disgust which the principles on which business is managed inspire, and turn drudges, or die of disgust, some of them suicides. What is the remedy? ...

Is it not the chief disgrace in the world, not to be an unit; not to be reckoned one character; not to yield that peculiar fruit which each man was created to bear, but to be reckoned in the gross, in the hundred, or the thousand, of the party, the section, to which we belong; and our opinion predicted geographically, as the north, or the south? Not so, brothers and friends—please God, ours shall not be so.

We will walk on our own feet; we will work with our own hands; we will speak our own minds. Then shall man be no longer a name for pity, for doubt, and for sensual indulgence. The dread of man and the love of man shall be a wall of defense and a wreath of joy around all. A nation of men will for the first time exist, because each believes himself inspired by the Divine Soul which also inspires all men.

---

*Son of a Unitarian minister, schooled at Boston Latin and Harvard,* RALPH WALDO EMERSON [1803-1882] *embodied the city's pivotal role in American thought. He spearheaded the* TRANSCENDENTALIST MOVEMENT, *a circle that included Henry David Thoreau, Margaret Fuller and many others. The Dial, the Transcendentalists' leading journal, debuted in 1840 with Fuller as editor. Focused on nature, individualism and Eastern thought, the movement still influences American bohemia and academia.*

# WHITEY BULGER

*The Irish American gangster James "Whitey" Bulger dominated organized crime in Boston for decades, running drugs, smuggling arms and orchestrating numerous murders. In 2013, after a long national manhunt, Bulger stood trial in Boston. In these excerpts from sworn testimony, Bulger associate Kevin Weeks describes a hit.*

Jim Bulger showed up at the club. He was in the "tow truck." That's — there was a boiler hit car that we had. We had to use the code name "tow truck," so if anyone heard us talking about it, they'd just think it was a tow truck.

It was a '75 Malibu. It was all souped up. And it was equipped with a smoke screen, and, you know, an oil slick we'd lay down. You could drive it at night with the rear lights out. It was a hit car.

He had put a wig on, and he had a floppy mustache on.

He handed me a police scanner. He handed me a radio, a two-way radio. And he told me where Brian was sitting in the Pier restaurant, and, "Go down there and watch him, and let me know when he's coming out."

Brian Halloran, "Balloon Head." He had a big head. We got word that he was cooperating with the FBI on a couple of murders.

So I went down and parked across the street in Anthony's Pier 4 in the parking lot, and I looked through the binoculars and waited for Brian Halloran. I could see him sitting there in a booth and—just a table by the window. And then when he got up, I picked up the two-way radio and I said, "The Balloon's Rising." And I repeated it a couple of times. Then when he came outside, I said, "The Balloon's in the air." And then a little blue car, a Datsun, pulled up, and Brian Halloran got in the passenger side.

Then Jim Bulger pulled in with the "tow truck," and he was facing in, and the Datsun was facing out. So he slid across the front seat and he yelled out, "Brian," and he started to proceed to start shooting.

People were screaming. Eventually, the car that Michael Donahue was driving just drifted across the road and kind of bumped on the other side in front of—I think it was called the Port O'Call or something. It was a restaurant there. It's now Whiskey Priest. And Jim Bulger made a U-turn, came back around, and Brian Halloran had exited the vehicle.

As he walked toward the rear of his vehicle, he actually was walking right towards where Jim Bulger was parked, you know, in the street. And Jim Bulger just started shooting right at him.

Brian Halloran went down, and Jim Bulger kept on shooting him, and his body was bouncing off the ground.

# THE T

*The spokes of Boston's venerable subway carry meaning in their names.*

ORANGE LINE

Adjacent to Washington Street, which was originally called Orange Street. **STOPS:** Chinatown, Back Bay, Roxbury Crossing, Oak Grove.

RED LINE

Travels through crimson-hued Harvard. **STOPS:** Davis, Harvard, Kendall/MIT, Broadway.

GREEN LINE

Runs along the famed Emerald Necklace parks. **STOPS:** Park Street, Boston University Central, North Station, Boston College.

BLUE LINE

Named for the water it travels beneath, Boston Harbor. **STOPS:** Revere Beach, Suffolk Downs, Aquarium, Government Center.

> *The design firm* CAMBRIDGE SEVEN ASSOCIATES *introduced the line names as part of a 1965 visual overhaul, which also enshrined Helvetica as the T's signage font of choice.*

# IMPORTS

The Boston Evening Post, *January 2, 1769*

IMPORTED in the laſt Ships from LONDON And to be Sold by Henry Laughton At his Store the corner of School ſtreet near the Rev'd Doctor Sewall's Meeting: A good Aſſortment of Engliſh Goods, Suitable for the Season; among which are, A variety of ſuperfine, middling and low pric'd Broad-Cloths, plain & napt Bath-Beavers, Bearſkins, green, blue and cloth coloured Ratteens, German ſerges, Lambſkins for Surtouts, with all forts of Trimming ſuitable, Camblets, plain & ſtrip'd Cambleteens, figur'd & ſtrip'd Stuffs, Grizetts, Poplins, Diamantines, Calimancoes, ſuper-fine ſcarlet Whitneys, coarſe red & blue do. Flannel, ſtrip'd & plain Swanſkins, plain & ſtrip'd Duffils, Colecheſter & Drapery Baizes, Gold & Silver Baſket Buttons, Gold & Silver Lace, Thread & Vellum, Choice Bohea Tea & Indigo, with a Variety of other Woollen & India Goods, cheap for Caſh.

# JULIA CHILD

*The culinary icon lived in Cambridge from 1961 to 2001.*
*A tour of her gustatory geography.*

BOSTON UNIVERSITY  Julia co-founded BU's gastronomy master's program with Jacques Pépin. *Fenway-Kenmore*

SAVENOR'S BUTCHER & MARKET  She shopped here often, befriending owner Jack Savenor. *Cambridge*

HARVEST  One of Julia's favorite restaurants, located in Harvard Square. A go-to order: cast-iron liver and onions. *Cambridge*

LEGAL SEA FOODS  Julia favored the original Inman Square location, since burned down, but this local mini-chain is going strong. *Cambridge*

WGBH  *The French Chef* transformed U.S. home cooks' ambitions and repertoire. The public TV icon's members can now stream episodes for a refresher on her joyous abandon. *Brighton*

103 IRVING STREET  Her house, original location for her now-famous kitchen, since deconstructed and installed at the Smithsonian in D.C. *Cambridge*

..................................................................................................

### "Making Dinner at Julia's"
*Washington Post*, April 13, 1983

Julia Child never misses a beat as she confides to the unseen audience, "It looks awful at this point, which is normal." She covers the pan to let it simmer, takes a break to watch the tape and give it a hearty laugh, then returns to the stove to fuss over the caramel as the crew swirl around her. The pears are done but the tape needs reloading, so there is an emergency call for "more sizzle." The segment ends with Child arranging puff pastry, caramel, pastry cream, pears and whipped cream on a plate—but not without endless retakes of rearranged pastry tops and conferences over the placement of whipped cream, not to mention drips of caramel on the plate. She wipes off a drip with her finger and licks it, asking if anyone has seen her purple towel so that she could wipe it the way chef Henry Haller does it in the White House. "I wish we were going to get him. Do you think we could get him?" she wonders.

# CITY UPON A HILL

John Winthrop
"A Model of Christian Charity"
Holyrood Church, Southampton, England, March 1630

We must delight in each other; make others' conditions our own; rejoice together, mourn together, labor and suffer together, always having before our eyes our commission and community in the work, as members of the same body. So shall we keep the unity of the spirit in the bond of peace. The Lord will be our God, and delight to dwell among us, as His own people, and will command a blessing upon us in all our ways, so that we shall see much more of His wisdom, power, goodness and truth, than formerly we have been acquainted with. We shall find that the God of Israel is among us, when ten of us shall be able to resist a thousand of our enemies; when He shall make us a praise and glory that men shall say of succeeding plantations, "may the Lord make it like that of New England." For we must consider that we shall be as a city upon a hill. The eyes of all people are upon us. So that if we shall deal falsely with our God in this work we have undertaken, and so cause Him to withdraw His present help from us, we shall be made a story and a by-word through the world. We shall open the mouths of enemies to speak evil of the ways of God, and all professors for God's sake. We shall shame the faces of many of God's worthy servants, and cause their prayers to be turned into curses upon us till we be consumed out of the good land whither we are going.

*The address to Massachusetts Bay's first colonists was long neglected but now figures as a staple of American rhetoric. For a modern assessment, see* City on a Hill: A History of American Exceptionalism *by Abram C. Van Engen.*

## THE ATLANTIC

Must be said that most publishing-world dinner parties don't lead to much. But one night in 1857, a few of the boys got together—Longfellow, Emerson, Oliver Wendell Holmes, that crowd. They gabbed about a magazine. And, in a rare move, they really did start one. *The Atlantic* has shaped American discourse ever since, forever bearing the stamp of its Boston birth: forward-thinking, contentious at times, forever abuzz with ideas. With a byline roster running from Twain to Wharton to Coates, the conversation hasn't flagged yet.

## PAUL REVERE

*In spring 1775, relations between colonists and British troops occupying Boston reached a breaking point. A British foray against the self-declared Provincial Congress and colonist arms caches sent one local silversmith on a night of epic adventure.*

APRIL 18, 1775. 10 P.M. British troops muster on Boston Common, alarming patriots including Dr. Joseph Warren. Warren summons Paul Revere and sends him to warn militias and leaders outside Boston, particularly Provincial Congress notables Samuel Adams and John Hancock, then in Lexington.

APPROX. 11 P.M. Revere instructs Robert Newman, Old North Church sexton, to light two lanterns in the steeple, prearranged signal to Charlestown of British operations by water. Revere crosses to Charlestown, mounts up and rides into the night.

AROUND MIDNIGHT Revere rouses a militia captain in Medford and "alarm[s] almost every house" on his route. Warning: "The Regulars are coming out."

APRIL 19, 12:30 A.M. At the Lexington home of Rev. Jonas Clarke, Revere parleys with Hancock and Adams. Other riders dispatched, signals sent: an "alarm and muster" system developed for crisis moments.

1:30 A.M. Revere, along with riders William Dawes and Dr. Samuel Prescott, alerts countryside west of Boston. British patrol captures Revere, others flee.

2:30 A.M. Nearing Lexington, British detachment spooked by gunshot, other noise, releases Revere and withdraws to warn main group of troops.

3:30 A.M. Revere reaches Hancock and Adams by foot and assists them in fleeing from Lexington. Meanwhile, a militia company has gathered at Buckman Tavern.

4 A.M. Revere sent to Buckman Tavern for important documents. Military action around Boston makes his return to the city impossible. He ultimately boards at Waterton.

APPROX. 5 A.M. British troops confront militia on Lexington Green. Single shot sparks skirmish. Eight militiamen, one British soldier killed, triggering running battles in Lexington, Concord and Boston's environs. American Revolution begins.

## THE SPORTS PAGES

*Every city believes it's the greatest sports town.
Boston's case is stronger than most. The sporting
heritage here embraces the ring and road, the field
and court, stirring a pride that stands apart.*

---

### BOSTON MARATHON

*The Patriot's Day race from Hopkinton to Boylston Street is Boston's great sporting
festival, known for huge crowds and infamous hills. Five great editions:*

**SALAZAR/BEARDSLEY** [1982] The "Duel in the Sun." Alberto Salazar and
Dick Beardsley battle for miles. Raucous crowds. Salazar's relentless drafting
pays off with a last-mile pass; Beardsley's desperate sprint falls short.

...................................................................................................

**BROWN/KELLEY** [1936] On the Newton Hills' crushing final climb,
Medford boy John Kelley catches Ellison "Tarzan" Brown, Narragansett
tribal member from Rhode Island. Kelley gives Brown a pat as he passes.
Brown then rallies and wins. "Heartbreak Hill" gets its name.

...................................................................................................

**BOBBI GIBB** [1966] Defying sexist ban, avid runner Roberta Gibb Bingay
jumps out of the bushes at the start, finishes in top half. *Sports Illustrated*:
"How jarring an effect Mrs. Bingay's example of feminine endurance had
on countless male egos can easily be guessed."

...................................................................................................

**BENOIT/RODGERS** [1979] The American '70s running boom peaks with
double American wins by New England heroes: "Boston Billy" Rodgers
and Bowdoin senior Joan Benoit.

...................................................................................................

**DESI LINDEN** [2018] A "blue-collar" runner beloved by Boston fans solos to
the line in the rain, the first victorious American woman in decades.

# FIGHTERS OF NOTE

### JOHN L. SULLIVAN *"The Boston Strongboy"*

Bare knuckles or gloves, Roxbury's son crushed 1880s–1890s rivals.
America's first sporting star. Nellie Bly in 1889: "If John L. Sullivan isn't
able to whip any pugilist in the world, I would like to see the man who is."

.................................................................

### ROCKY MARCIANO *"The Brockton Blockbuster"*

Forty-nine bouts, 49 wins, 43 KOs. The Rock achieved 1950s icon
status with "the force of a meteor slamming into earth" [fight writer
Bernard Fernandez]. Dead at 45: Iowa plane crash.

.................................................................

### KENNY FLORIAN *"KenFlo"*

Arguably the brainiest, most versatile of Boston's modern mixed
martial arts crop. Makes all the "greats with no titles" lists.

.................................................................

### SAM LANGFORD *"The Boston Bonecrusher"*

Canadian-born Black fighter. Devastating punch. Stymied by early
1900s racism, declared honorary world champ in 2020.

.................................................................

### JACK SHARKEY *"The Boston Gob"*

Lithuanian immigrant, 1920s hardman. Grew up a fisherman, catching
bass barehanded. Learned the fight game in Navy brawls.

.................................................................

### MARVELOUS MARVIN HAGLER

His legal name. Brockton-reared southpaw, classed among middleweight
greats by *The Ring* and others. An '80s belt winner, he died in early 2021.

---

## THE PASS

*Boston College 41, University of Miami 45. Six seconds remaining.*

"Three wide receivers out to the right. Flutie flushed. Throws it down.
CAUGHT BY BOSTON COLLEGE! I DON'T BELIEVE IT! IT'S A
TOUCHDOWN! THE EAGLES WIN IT! I DON'T BELIEVE IT!
Phelan is at the bottom of that pile. Here comes the Boston College team.
He threw it into the end zone! There was no time left on the clock! The
ball went between two defensive backs of Miami! Doug Flutie has done it!"

—*Brent Musburger, CBS, November 23, 1984*

## TOM BRADY

*In 2000, the New England Patriots selected a Michigan quarterback as the NFL draft's 199th pick. Tom Brady became arguably—or, in Boston, inarguably—the greatest QB ever. Highlights from the original scouting report from draft expert Mel Kiper:*

"Smart, experienced big-game signal-caller, getting very high grades in the efficiency department this past season."

"He's not going to try to force the action, rarely trying to perform beyond his capability."

"At the pro level, his lack of mobility could surface as a problem, and it will be interesting to see how he fares when forced to take more changes down the field."

"Sure, he doesn't have the total package of skills ..."

## THE 2004 PLAYOFFS

Before it became a Titletown, before duck boat championship parades came with every changing season, Boston carried a curse. In 1918, baseball's Red Sox won a third World Series in four seasons. But the next year, the club dealt star Babe Ruth to the New York Yankees for a proverbial bag of balls. The Bronx Bombers would go on to win championships by the literal dozen. Boston would acquire zero titles and an inferiority complex. Breaking the Curse of the Bambino, a term coined by local sports columnist Dan Shaughnessy, seemed to require cosmic intervention. Enter a freewheeling band of self-proclaimed idiots. Following a heartbreaking loss to the hated Yanks in the 2003 American League Championship Series, the 2004 Red Sox coalesced around stars—David Ortiz, Pedro Martinez, Manny Ramirez, Johnny Damon—whose casually clutch performances and shaggy personae charmed buttoned-up Boston. In a bit of symmetry only Hollywood could script, the club would find itself in an ALCS sequel against New York. This time, trailing 3-0 in the series, moments from elimination, the Red Sox rallied. Game-winning blasts from Ortiz and the bloody sock of pitcher Curt Schilling live forever in Boston lore. It was baseball's first-ever series comeback from a 3-0 deficit. A clean World Series sweep of the Cardinals officially banished the hex on the team and the city's psyche.

# THE BOSTON RED SOX

*Founded in 1901, the baseball club symbolizes Boston's affinity for tradition and underdog struggle. An all-time lineup, eclectically chosen:*

**LEFT FIELD** Ted Williams [1939–1960] *"Boston and Ted Williams … has been a marriage, composed of spats, mutual disappointments, and, toward the end, a mellowing hoard of shared memories." —John Updike*

...............................................................................................................

**CENTER FIELD** Tris Speaker [1907–1915] *Anchored "Million Dollar Outfield," won two World Series. Later, an innovative manager.*

...............................................................................................................

**RIGHT FIELD** Manny Ramirez [2001–2008] *Wacky eye of the storm in title-winning redemption era. [Rare stint in RF makes room for Ted.]*

...............................................................................................................

**FIRST BASE** Carl Yastrzemski [1961–1983] *Sorry, Jimmie Foxx, Mo Vaughn, et al. Sox lifer Yaz has to play somewhere.*

...............................................................................................................

**SECOND BASE** Pumpsie Green [1959–1962] *The first Black player for the last major-league team to integrate.*

...............................................................................................................

**SHORT STOP** Nomar Garciaparra [1996–2004] *An iconic figure in turn-of-this-century New England. Ask a native to say his name.*

...............................................................................................................

**THIRD BASE** Wade Boggs [1982–1992] *Perennial All-Star with swashbuckling aura. Noted for claiming to drink 100 beers in a day [largely substantiated].*

...............................................................................................................

**RIGHT-HANDED PITCHER** Pedro Martinez [1998–2004] *Dominant run in Boston had the perfect ending: World Series glory.*

...............................................................................................................

**LEFT-HANDED PITCHER** Babe Ruth [1914–1919] *Brash young hurler with some power at the plate. Sale to Yankees allegedly summoned curse.*

...............................................................................................................

**CATCHER** Carlton Fisk [1969, 1971–1980] *1975 World Series Game 6 dinger: permanent YouTube dopamine dose.*

...............................................................................................................

**DESIGNATED HITTER** David Ortiz [2003–2016] *Big Papi. An infectious presence made him a city legend.*

...............................................................................................................

**PINCH RUNNER** Dave Roberts [2004] *Auteur of greatest stolen base ever, 2004 ALCS: perfect jump, perfect slide, storied comeback unlocked.*

## THE BOSTON BRUINS

1924..... Grocer Charles Adams launches NHL's first U.S. team

1929..... Bruins win first Stanley Cup. Tiny Thompson in goal behind "Dynamite Line."

1939..... "Sudden Death" Mel Hill scores three overtime playoff goals

1942..... World War II: Key players join Royal Canadian Air Force
...... NHL shrinkage leaves Boston as one of so-called Original Six

1948.... Wiretap reveals young star Don Gallinger's game-fixing schemes. Lifetime ban.

1954..... Boston becomes first NHL team to deploy a Zamboni

1958..... Willie O'Ree skates the wing: first Black NHL player

1966..... Bobby Orr debuts. Club hero for 10 seasons. Arguably the GOAT.

1967..... Ventures instrumental song "Nutty" becomes broadcast signature

1970..... Phil Esposito and Orr lead Bruins to first Stanley Cup in 29 years

1971..... Esposito scores 76 goals, a record that stands till Gretzky
.... Terry "Bloody" O'Reilly drafted: captain, all-time penalty leader

1979..... Defenseman Ray Bourque begins storied 21-year Bruins career
..... Mike Milbury pummels New York Rangers fan with fan's own shoe. Please go watch this golden footage.

1988..... Boston Garden lights fail during Stanley Cup game

1997..... Three-decade run of playoff appearances ends

2003..... Dropkick Murphys release Bruins tribute song "Time to Go"

2006..... Zdeno Chára, towering Slovak with warp-speed shot, joins up

2010..... Bruins host outdoor game at Fenway. Stirring overtime win.

2011..... Victory over Vancouver Canucks gives Boston first Cup in 39 years

2020..... Presidents' Trophy for COVID year's best regular season

---

BOBBY ORR *ended the 1970 Stanley Cup with an overtime goal against the St. Louis Blues. Photographer Ray Lussier of the Boston Record American turned the play into hockey's most famous image: Orr sailing through the air, already celebrating, no helmet. According to legend, Lussier got the shot only because another photographer had bolted for a beer. The paper reported: "His teammates swarmed him and fell on him. Sinden came skidding out to join the celebration. So did a swarm of youngsters. The ice was littered with hats, streamers, beer cans, cups, papers, and a lot of other bric-a-brac."*

# BOSTON CELTICS

*Writerly insight on classic Celts.*

### BOB COUSY [1950–1963]

"This was how Houdini became Houdini: He slung the ball sidearm sixty feet downcourt, and to the streaking teammate who received it, the ball seemed to have wings and a homing device. On the fast break, he cupped the ball and faked a shot as he dropped it to a teammate behind him. He stared at a teammate as he passed the ball, or sometimes he looked the other way. His passes had zip, curve, careful measure, and purpose."

—*Gary M. Pomerantz,* The Last Pass

### PAUL PIERCE [1998–2013]

"Whenever the team is locked in, and he knows it, he starts carrying himself a little differently. Puffs his chest out, turns to his bench after baskets to feed off their reactions, struts around during stoppages doing his 'nodding and staring down the crowd' routine. Puts his swagger suit on, basically. His backbreaking 3 with 2:47 remaining didn't surprise me in the least, nor did his reaction afterward—the slow jog backward, the prolonged stare at his bench, the nodding that always comes with it."

—*Bill Simmons,* Grantland

### LARRY BIRD [1979–1992]

"On the road the crowd comes early to the games, and the people—not just little kids and teenagers but grown men and women—throng around the Celtics basket, wanting to be near the Rookie, hoping to see, even in the warmup, something singular. The Rookie is aware of this, but he withholds his touch, even his look. He wills his eyes not to see them. He is comfortable within himself only as a basketball player, never as a showman, and so he is deliberately restrained. There will be nothing flamboyant in the warmup."

—*David Halberstam,* Inside Sports

---

*Winner of 11 championships with the Celtics' 1960s dynasty,*
BILL RUSSELL *was known for social-justice ethics and forbidding personal affect. In 1979, he described himself: "I used the glower ... a big batch of smoldering Black Panther, a touch of Lord High Executioner and angry Cyclops mixed together, with just a dash of the old Sonny Liston."*

---

# MAPS

Pictorial journeys through unique Boston
culture, commerce and landscapes by local illustrator
Julia Emiliani. Not to scale.

# THE Revolution

**Bunker Hill Monument**

**Liberty Tree**

**Roxbury High Fort**

**George Middleton House**

Boston
Tea Party
Museum

Old South
Meeting
House

Dorchester
Heights

Thomas
Hutchinson
House

# THE REVOLUTION

*Tension between Yankee liberties and British rule boiled over on Boston's streets, forever marking the city as the Revolution's hometown.*

### THE LIBERTY TREE SITE

Fire your mind to picture the elm where patriots [and street gangs] rallied against the 1760s Stamp Act. A national emblem predating those stars and stripes. *Washington and Essex streets*

### OLD SOUTH MEETING HOUSE

Rebel Boston's biggest church, ground zero for debate. A 1768 rally against British Navy actions triggered military occupation. *310 Washington St*

### THOMAS HUTCHINSON HOUSE SITE

Stamp Act–riled rioters sacked the governor's house in 1765: "Hellish crew with the Rage of devils." *Hanover St, near Paul Revere House*

### BOSTON TEA PARTY SHIPS & MUSEUM

Touristy? Sure, but great, too. Costumed re-enactors protest against taxed tea, a vivid hint of 1773's populist anger and tumult. *306 Congress St*

### GEORGE MIDDLETON HOUSE

This is a post-Revolution structure, but one of Beacon Hill's oldest. Built by the leader of an all-Black Revolutionary militia. *5 Pinckney St*

### ROXBURY HIGH FORT

After Lexington and Concord, Colonial forces besieged the Brits in Boston. Earthworks here played a key role. *Beech Glen St and Fort Ave*

### BUNKER HILL MONUMENT

A prominent obelisk and excellent museum mark scenes of fierce combat as colonists tried to hold the high ground against well-trained British troops. *Monument Square, Charlestown*

### DORCHESTER HEIGHTS

Washington's forces seized high ground in March 1776 and carted in heavy artillery captured in New York by Benedict Arnold, others. Brits fled the city. *Thomas Park*

---

FREE CITY *Historian Mark Peterson's* The City-State of Boston [2019] *paints a fascinating portrait of Boston as an independent force of change—almost a nation of its own.*

# FENWAY PARK

*Home of the Olde Towne Team and a major-league shrine,*
*the 1912 ballpark holds many curiosities.*

### GREEN MONSTER

Originally built to block rubber-
neckers, Fenway's signature wall
grew 37 feet tall after a fire. Funky
caroms haunt opposing fielders
and pitchers. Monster-top seats
fetch top dollar. *Left field*

### SCOREBOARD

A scorekeeper manually swaps out
crooked numbers, working in a
smelly cavern where autographs
adorn the walls. *Left field*

### BLEACHER BAR

No tickets? No problem.
This sidewalk-accessible watering
hole offers prime heckling
opportunities via a garage window
below the center field stands.
*82A Lansdowne St*

### RED SEAT

A painted chair honors the park's
longest round-tripper: a 502-foot
homer struck by Ted Williams
in 1946. Ricocheted off a straw
hat. *Section 42, Row 37, Seat 21*

### PESKY'S POLE

Named for a beloved infielder
short on power, the right field foul
pole stakes one end of the park's
oddly shaped outfield, just 302
feet from home plate: the shortest
home run distance in the big
leagues. *Right field*

### GARDENS

A previously unused strip of
roof now generates about 6,000
pounds of produce each season,
from kale to carrots to Swiss
chard. Relief pitchers grow
tomatoes from their post beyond
the outfield fence. *Third-base line,*
*bullpen*

### JERSEY STREET

Two bustling blocks, formerly
known as Yawkey Way but re-
named in 2018 to distance the
club from racism under late owner
Tom Yawkey. [The Sox were the
last MLB club to field a Black
player.] Swarm here for souvenirs.
*Between Gates A and D*

---

GREEN GUIDE *David R. Mellor oversees the elaborate designs mowed into*
*the Fenway outfield. See his book* Picture Perfect: Mowing Techniques
for Lawns, Landscapes, and Sports, *the "textbook" for lawn patterns.*

LONGFELLOW BRIDGE

SUNSET CRUISE

HATCH SHELL

CHARLES RIVER BIKE PATH

# CHARLES RIVER

*This 80-mile-long waterway is Boston's figurative artery
but a very literal place to get the blood pumping.*

### CHARLES RIVER ESPLANADE

This 64-acre riverfront park is where you'll find perfect picnic spots, public art, recreational areas, playgrounds, cute dogs and that cinematic running route you've long pictured. *esplanade.org*

### WELD BOATHOUSE

Picturesque home to Harvard's varsity women's rowing crews, the halfway point of the Head of the Charles Regatta course.
*971 Memorial Dr, Cambridge*

### LONGFELLOW BRIDGE

Known to locals as the Salt-and-Pepper Shaker Bridge [thanks to its granite towers], the official name honors local poet Henry Wadsworth Longfellow. *Beacon Hill to Cambridge*

### KAYAK RENTALS

Because sunny days do actually happen here. Boats hire out for one-way and round-trip jaunts. *paddleboston.com*

### HATCH SHELL

Spring through fall, this art deco outdoor amphitheater hosts concerts, films and other events, notably the Boston Pops orchestra on July 4. *hatchshell.com*

### SUNSET CRUISE

Sightsee, maybe with a cocktail in hand. A building-tour version features insight from Boston Society for Architecture. *charlesriverboat.com*

### MASSACHUSETTS AVENUE BRIDGE

Stretching 364.4 Smoots, this bridge was measured by one Oliver Smoot in 1958 when pledging an MIT frat. He laid down as Lambda Chi Alpha marked every 5 feet, 7 inches [his height]. *Back Bay to Cambridge*

### CHARLES RIVER BIKE PATH

Saddle up for the 22.9-mile route. Sights include the Museum of Science, campus architecture and geese, many geese. *traillink.com*

---

**SAIL AWAY** *For a quick but rigorous introduction to local waterways, enlist in Community Boating's two-lesson course, which leaves pupils ready to sail Mercury-class vessels.* community-boating.org

# BOSTON'S BRAIN

*With more than 40 higher-ed institutions,*
*Greater Boston offers many chances to get wicked smaht, kid.*

### BOSTON ATHENÆUM

This Nathaniel Hawthorne hangout combines the ethos of a public library with great works of science, art and literature. One speciality: American manuscripts and books *10½ Beacon St*

.................................................

### PÉPIN LECTURE SERIES

Celeb chef Jacques Pépin, co-founder of Boston University's gastronomy master's program, lends his name to a free lecture series *725 Commonwealth Ave*

.................................................

### THE RED ROOM AT CAFE 939

This intimate, 200-person Berklee venue showcases the music school's talent alongside alumni like Betty Who and stars like Leon Bridges. *939 Boylston St*

.................................................

### EMERSON COLLEGE MEDIA ART GALLERY

Contemporary gallery, featuring immersive, sometimes site-specific exhibitions featuring moving images, performance art and emergent media. *25 Avery St*

### STATA CENTER

Also known as Building 32, this MIT master class in catawampus architecture was designed in 2004 by Frank Gehry. Survived a 2007 lawsuit alleging dangerously flawed design. Noam Chomsky's place of work. *32 Vassar St, Cambridge*

.................................................

### HASTY PUDDING CLUB

One of Harvard's first social clubs began in 1795 as a way for students to avoid unsavory dining hall food but quickly evolved into a satirical tradition of roasts, burlesque shows and other productions. *45 Dunster St, Cambridge*

.................................................

### HIP-HOP ARCHIVE

Located at UMass Boston's Joseph P. Healey Library, this collection of all things Boston hip-hop started in 2016 with recordings from the local radio show *Lecco's Lemma,* hosted by the eccentric Magnus Johnstone.
*100 Morrissey Blvd*

---

ALMA MATER *You could make a good argument for Harvard Yard as the epicenter of American learning. The university offers history-focused tours of its venerable core.* harvard.edu/visit

STATA
CENTER

BOSTON
ATHENAEUM

UMASS
HIP-HOP
ARCHIVE

RED'S BEST

EAST BOSTON OYSTERS

LA PESCHERIA
EATALY'S SEAFOOD COUNTER

B&G OYSTERS

# SEAFOOD

*From top-notch sashimi to no-frills clam chowder,
Bostonians know how to enjoy the fruits of the sea.*

### EAST BOSTON OYSTERS

Dedicated to making oysters and caviar more approachable, EBO throws fun pop-up parties in unlikely [and secret] places in East Boston and beyond. *eastbostonoysters.com*

### SALTIE GIRL

Hot and buttered or cold with mayo, there's nothing more Boston than a lobster roll. Saltie Girl does it best. Amazing tinned fish lineup, too. 281 *Dartmouth St*

### LEGAL SEA FOODS

Fire took out the original Inman Square spot, where Julia Child enjoyed fresh catch on paper plates. Today's Kendall Square location embodies a 70-year-old institution. 355 *Main St, Cambridge*

### RED'S BEST

For a quality cup of clam chowdah, there's only one place to go: the Red's Best stall in Boston Public Market. 100 *Hanover St*

### EATALY

Come for the cheese and salumi, stay for the pescivendolo. Fishmongers source the freshest fish from local, sustainable fishermen and distributors like Island Creek Oysters and Red's Best. 800 *Boylston St*

### B&G OYSTERS

South Boston native and chef Barbara Lynch, noted for restaurants all over town, serves up regional bivalves [Abigail Pearls, Moondancers] and other New England staples at this South End neighborhood joint. 550 *Tremont St*

### CAFE SUSHI

This family-run sushi spot has crafted the best Japanese raw delicacies in Boston since 1984. Splurge on the omakase menu or choose your own nigiri- and sashimi-filled adventure. Gyoza and excellent salads bail out any landlocked taste buds in the house. 1105 *Massachusetts Ave, Cambridge*

---

FISH FEST *The Boston Seafood Festival may be newish, debuting in 2012, but its setting evokes seafood heritage. The summer bash on century-old Fish Pier benefits sustainability.* bostonfisheriesfoundation.org

# IRISH BARS

*By every count America's most Irish city, Boston says* sláinte *in many different accents, rough-edged to high-brow.*

### J.J. FOLEY'S CAFE

Open since 1909, this South End establishment lays claim to the title of oldest family-run Irish pub in Boston. Ancient posters and a plaque marking a 1919 police strike back it up. *117 E Berkeley St*

### THE BLACK ROSE

Authenticity where you'd least expect it. In the shadow of Faneuil Hall, immigrant brogues and tourist chatter mingle within a 45-year-old bar known for nightly live Irish music. *160 State St*

### L STREET TAVERN

Passersby might not recognize the *Good Will Hunting* setting anymore—renovations have altered its facade—but an inviting space draws in movie enthusiasts and locals anyway. *658 E 8th St*

### THE PLOUGH AND STARS

This heady corner between MIT and Harvard has attracted many scribes over the years, including poet Seamus Heaney. Its name inspired the title for *Ploughshares*, an eminent local lit journal. *912 Massachusetts Ave, Cambridge*

### THE BURREN

Tufts students and older locals make for raucous nights at a bar with one of the area's best live music scenes and rowdiest back rooms. *247 Elm St, Somerville*

### BRENDAN BEHAN PUB

A Jamaica Plain staple offers an impressive tap lineup, a laid-back vibe that suits the neighborhood and a menu that's a delightfully odd mashup of cheap hot dogs and empanadas. *378 Centre St*

### SULLIVAN'S TAP

Unlike the large sports bars in its vicinity, this dive makes do with a narrow space near the Celtics' and Bruins' Garden home. An extraordinarily long bar means a pint's just a shuffleboard slide away. *168 Canal St*

---

IRISH TIMES  *For chatty, newsy coverage of Boston, the diaspora and politics across the Atlantic, track down a copy of quarterly newspaper* Boston Irish. bostonirish.com

# IRISH BARS

J.J.FOLEY'S

The Black Rose

BRENDAN BEHAN PUB

THE PLOUGH & STARS

THE BURREN

Sullivan's Tap

L ST. TAVERN INC. LIGHT LUNCH L ST. TAVERN

L ST TAVERN

# INTERVIEWS

Twelve conversations with locals of note about growing up in Boston, moving to Boston, watching the waterfront, running the streets and restoring venerable art.

# ELLE SIMONE SCOTT

*CHEF, FOOD STYLIST*

**I WAS BASICALLY** scouted, if you will, by *America's Test Kitchen* to be their food stylist. You can't do that remotely, so I moved from New York.

**I SUBLET A** cute studio apartment right on Newbury Street, in Back Bay. Totally my Boston *Sex in the City* moment.

**THE FIRST TIME** it hit me was when I had seafood. Specifically clam chowder. The first time I'd ever had real New England clam chowder, not from a can.

**I'D NEVER CARED** for it. But what I had that day, it blew my mind. *Whoa, this is what real seafood tastes like.*

**I'VE DEFINITELY FOUND** community among the women in the culinary industry here.

**THE AMERICA'S TEST KITCH-EN** crew became my first, immediate family. And then I got diagnosed with ovarian cancer after starting the job.

**THEY JUST KIND** of kicked into gear, doing what family members do.

**ONE OF THE** things I love most about Boston food media is that it's not an oversaturated market—especially compared to New York, which is so saturated for every freaking thing.

**IF YOU SAY,** "Hey, I'd like to write for your publication," most of the time the response is, "Cool, what do you want to write about?" There's just a lot of room to provide new perspectives.

**YOU GET TO** talk about gender equality and racial inequality in so many varying ways. Boston has a reputation, but folks in food and media don't *want* that reputation. They're open to diverse voices.

**I KNOW WHAT** it's like to be from a place and feel like you're just rolling with the punches. Sometimes it's easier for an outsider to tap that vein.

# MICHAEL LAUB

*BIOLOGT PROFESSOR*

**BOSTON IS WHERE** you want to be if you're a biologist. There's really nowhere else like it on the planet. The concentration is just unprecedented.

**THERE'S THIS HUGE** academic world: Harvard, MIT. Then you also have all these world-class hospitals. On top of that, you have an amazing biotech industry, especially in Kendall Square. Just this explosion of companies—Big Pharma, but also all sorts of start-ups. A whole biology ecosystem, if you will.

**YOU CAN ALWAYS** find an expert. If your research takes some new direction and you need to find someone who's an expert in it, they're in town.

**A CLASS OF** viruses infect bacteria, called bacteriophage, or "phage" for short.

**IN MY LAB,** we study mechanisms bacteria use to make themselves immune, or defend themselves against viral predators. It's amazing that bacteria have all these mechanisms.

**I GREW UP** in California, did grad school at Stanford. I'd considered Boston, actually, but at the time it was far too cold for my taste.

**I INTERVIEWED** for grad school at MIT—where I work now—in February. It dumped 6 inches of snow. I had my canvas Vans on. My feet were just frozen to the bone. Categorically off the list.

**NOW I TRY** to help students we recruit from California. We talk about, here's how to survive here, and why you should actually prefer to come here.

**WHEN IT WARMS** up, people just rejoice in a way they don't on the West Coast.

**MIT UNDERGRADS** are really fun to teach. They're a special group of people. No one goes to MIT as a backup school. They're fired up, passionate. You don't have to motivate them in any way.

# SOFI MADISON

*SHOP OWNER*

**I NEVER THOUGHT** I'd move back to Boston. No one ever does.

**IT'S THE HARSH** winters and the humid, sticky summers. And the pressure that comes from being in such a career-driven, education-driven city. I don't relate to that energy.

**I FIGURED IT** would be smart to open a soft spot in a city that felt a little rushed and competitive. A space that was warm and welcoming and vulnerable.

**WE OPENED** Olives & Grace in 2012. Our tagline is "a curtsy to the makers." The whole concept was to tip our hat to makers who do what they love and love what they do.

**WE REALLY APPRECIATE** the backstory: why a product is so important to bring to market.

**JUST LIKE WITH PEOPLE,** the same with products. If it looks good on the outside but doesn't have depth to it, it's not going to fly.

**THE SOUTH END IS,** far and away, my favorite neighborhood. The brownstones are so lovely and well protected and cared for. It doesn't get old to stroll these streets.

**I EAT HERE.** I drink here. I sit on the stoop and customers walk by. It's the whole *Sesame Street* experience.

**THERE'S A LOT** of smiling at strangers and knowing your neighbors. Going to the same restaurants week after week for years on end.

**FAMILIARITY IS A** really nice soil for our business to grow in.

**IT'S DEFINITELY** slower from a foot-traffic perspective, but you're getting the quality relationships.

**IN BOSTON,** at its finest, we look out for each other. We love to be regulars. We love to show love. I think we show love quite aggressively, which I find to be very charming and comical.

# TONY BARROS

*RESTAURANT OWNER*

**MY PARENTS IMMIGRATED** to the States in '76 and started bringing us over as small groups.

**WE USED TO** come through Portugal. There were no direct flights from Cape Verde. People would stay there for a month, two months before you got all your papers, ready to come.

**I WAS INVOLVED** in music a lot—Cape Verdean music. I used to DJ and promote club nights around Boston. I recorded a couple of albums.

**I ACTUALLY HAD** a dream once of a restaurant where you have dinner, and then after dinner, you just get up and dance in front of the DJ or a live band. Essentially, that's what we're doing now.

**PRETTY MUCH** every Cape Verdean artist has performed at Cesaria.

**THE FULL EXPERIENCE** of Cape Verde. The music, the drinks, the cuisine.

**AND ALSO,** the I-feel-at-home, friendly atmosphere.

**WE HAVE ONE** dish called *cachupa,* or stewed hominy. It's our national dish that we always try to make sure is on the menu. A hearty dish with pork. We make it with collard greens, beans, carrots. A lot of islands make their own versions.

**I KEEP SEEING** a lot of people move to the other areas of Massachusetts because housing is expensive. A lot of folks are buying properties in Brockton, New Bedford.

**WE GET PEOPLE** from all over the States and world. This is one of the places they want to experience. We are honored that we have been able to establish it as a landmark.

**WHENEVER IT'S NOT** too crazy busy or towards the end of the night, when things quiet down a little bit, I try to get onstage. I sing and play guitar.

# JOSEPH CHEEVERS

*POLICE SERGEANT*

**I GREW UP** in Dorchester. My mother worked with a telephone company. My father wasn't a fireman, but he worked for Boston Fire, at headquarters.

**THE HARBORMASTER JOB** was created in 1847 due to the chaos with shipping in those days. Boston was the closest port to Europe, the busiest port on the East Coast.

**SIX YEARS LATER,** 1853, the Boston police created the Harbor Patrol. Eventually the two merged, so harbormaster became a police position.

**I DID IT** for 10 years. I never knew exactly how busy the harbor is, 24 hours a day year-round, until I went to the Harbor Unit.

**IT'S THE ABSOLUTE** best job on the police department. Just to get out on the water, out along the Harbor Islands.

**PRE-9/11,** it was probably looked at as an old-age home.

Your last stop, three to five years before you retire. These days, it's everything but that.

**ON AN ANNUAL** basis, we pull probably anywhere from one to eight bodies out of the harbor. We've had bodies disappear for months, usually snagged on something when they went deep. It might take them awhile to shake loose.

**YOU WORK ON** the water all day. It can be very demanding, especially when it's hot.

**WE ONLY HAVE** two boats with air conditioning, so you could be in a very hot aluminum cabin all day. But you can't beat being on the water in the summertime.

**THE HARBOR ISLANDS** themselves are a hidden treasure. A lot of yacht clubs will pick an island to anchor off. Spectacle Island on a hot summer day, the temperature drops 10 to 15 degrees. It could be 90 in the city, 75 out around the Harbor Islands.

**MY CREW OFTEN** saw deer swimming from island to island.

**DEER EYES LIGHT** up, like other animals—they reflect light at nighttime.

**OR IF WE** have flare cameras on, we'll get a heat signature, something in the water.

**COYOTES SWIM.** There are coyotes on Spectacle Island for sure, and a good chance they're on Peddocks Island.

**THERE IS THE** occasional knucklehead who gets himself into trouble or gets somebody hurt due to their own negligence. A boater's responsible for their own wake. So if they shoot by a family in a canoe and overturn them, they're responsible for that type of behavior.

**IT'S NOT THE RICH,** yacht club–type life a lot of people envision. The average boater probably owns a 30-year-old boat with a 20-year-old engine.

**NOW I'M ASSIGNED** to a small security detail at City Hall. I live in South Boston, and I drive by the Harbor Unit every day to get to work.

**EVERY DAY IS** tough. I'm still close to all the officers that were assigned to the Harbor Patrol. I have occasionally done some overtime when they were short for different assignments, but it's not the same.

**MY GRANDPARENTS CAME** from Ireland. I love that part, the Irishness of Boston. I play the Highland bagpipes with the police pipe band. I was cofounder back in 1992. Normally a busy assignment. We typically do two or three events a week.

**I PROBABLY PRACTICED** more when I was assigned to the harbor. On the waterfront, there's not a lot of people around to complain about you playing bagpipes. There's nowhere to practice pipes at City Hall unless I go on the roof.

# ERIN ROBERTSON

*FASHION DESIGNER*

**I SEWED** in high school. My mom sewed. My grandma sewed. But it was never art. I saw it as home ec.

**ALSO,** my mom said, "Don't ever rely on a man to take care of you."

**I DIDN'T EVEN** know where Boston was on a map. I didn't know if it was a city or a state. I wasn't the smartest girl in Utah. Or really anywhere.

**MY DAD WASN'T** super around in my life, but he came at the right time. He knew what he was doing: getting his daughter out of Utah.

**I DID A** dental assistant course in high school, so I worked at Harvard dental school and private offices. I worked seven days a week for my first four years in Boston.

**I WENT TO** a Christmas party at this really cool production company. I remember thinking, *These people make art, and this is their office?*

**I APPLIED TO** MassArt when I was 24. It was like an itching inside of me.

**WHEN YOU THINK** through the lenses of science, art and design, you broaden what can happen.

**IT'S HARD TO** describe *Project Runway* just because of how absolutely intense it was.

**I'M THIS LITTLE** nugget from Provo. All of a sudden applying for *Project Runway*—and winning. I dealt with impostor syndrome.

**SOME PEOPLE WERE** raised for success. I was raised to be a housewife in a lot of ways.

**I TOOK A** class at MIT when I was a senior at MassArt. In that class, I was actually special because I was a fashion designer. Fashion is important.

**I LOVE STAYING** in Boston to stay connected to science. You have to imagine things that don't exist.

# SCOTT SURETTE

*PLUMBER*

**YOU NEVER SEEN** anybody work out of a shoebox before? That's my invoices in there. I hand-write my invoices.

**IT HAS TO** be at least an 11-and-a-half-size shoebox. That's my office.

**MY DAD DID** upholstery work. Seat covers, convertible tops. He also had a shop right in the Fenway area and used to park cars for Red Sox games. So kind of multitasking.

**FIVE BROTHERS,** one sister. All the brothers had their turn waving cars down the alley to get them to park for the ballgame.

**YOU GOT TO** capitalize.

**MY BROTHER MIKE** was working for a plumbing company out of Malden. They were looking for help, so I started with them back in '86.

**I'VE BEEN SELF-EMPLOYED** 26 years. Most of the work now is repeat.

**THE SAYING I** like best is, "Don't get dirty before 9:30, nothing new after 2." If you can live by that, that's a good thing. Not that it should reflect on my work ethic.

**BLUE COLLAR IS** paying more now. For trades and skilled labor, you can name your own price.

**ONE CUSTOMER** wanted me to have a Macallan with him, but it was only 11 o'clock in the morning.

**ONE CUSTOMER,** I cleaned his drain at a dentist office. He wanted to pay me with a bag of shrimp.

**ONE CUSTOMER,** she was just having a nasty smell in the toilet. She opened the lid and what she thought she saw—as I would confirm—was a dead squirrel.

**I DON'T KNOW** if she just left the lid open? They might have been going through her basement looking for something to drink. Yeah, it wasn't a good smell.

# HOLLY SALMON

*ART CONSERVATOR*

**ISABELLA STEWART** Gardner famously wrote in her will that her collection is to remain for the education and enjoyment of the public forever. Our team is responsible for the "forever" part.

**WE CARE FOR** all of the art, artifacts, decorative arts, furniture, paintings, frames, textiles, even the architecture.

**WE NEED TO** understand what a work of art is made of, how it was made. Scientific analysis is a big component. We're trained in art history, studio art and science—chemistry in particular, but also some physics.

**WE USE LASERS** that are typically used in the medical industry, for tattoo removal or wrinkle reduction. They're really great for cleaning a surface without causing damage.

**CLOSE LOOKING** is actually the most important tool. Spending a lot of time sitting in front of a work of art, looking.

**LIGHT EXPOSURE** and changes in temperature and relative humidity are very challenging for the structure of paper. And for the medium used on a paper surface, watercolors for instance.

**IN ANOTHER COLLECTION,** those very sensitive materials would be rotated off-view, put in storage, maybe shown every 5 to 10 years. But if you take a work of art off-view here, that leaves a hole in what Isabella intended you to see.

**I HAVE TO** say I spend a lot of my time trying to channel Isabella. What was she thinking? What would she want?

**I'VE WORKED HERE** for 18 years. I actually started my career here as a volunteer in college. And there's always discovery, something new we find in the process.

**FROM THE CHARLES,** you see the State House with its gold dome, and these low, historic brick buildings. And then behind that, the city rises up onto the horizon.

# MICHAEL PATRICK MACDONALD

*AUTHOR*

**WHEN I WROTE** *All Souls,* people would ask, "How did you find your voice?" That's a common question for writers. To answer, I have to go way back, 10 years before the book came out.

**THE LOWER END,** as we called it, included three census tracts with the highest concentration of white poverty in America.

**THEY HELD THE** projects, but also a lot of vinyl-sided houses stuck together.

**ALL SOULS,** my first memoir, tells the story of growing up in that neighborhood. It was insular, isolated.

**AFTER BUSING,** which initially applied only to the poorest white neighborhood and the poorest Black neighborhood, the walls between South Boston and the world went up.

**WE WERE DUPED** by racist politicians and their relatives in organized crime.

**BULGER'S** headquarters were just outside the projects. Right on the edge of a really vulnerable population.

**A PRIME POPULATION** to recruit for bank robberies, for the drug trade, as consumers of the drug trade.

**I WAS ONE** of 11 kids raised by a single mother. She lost four children to violence connected to drugs and crime.

**THE BOOK'S ALSO** about the work I needed to do by crossing the bridge to the so-called enemy neighborhood of Roxbury.

**I SPENT THE** better part of a decade doing community organizing on all the issues that affected my family in the projects. Violence, crime, substance abuse. In our case, organized crime. A lot of violent young deaths.

**COMING FROM SOUTHIE,** there was no such thing as community organizing. You'd be chased out of town as a communist. I had to go to other places in Boston.

...........................................................

**SOME OF THE** best friends of my life—mentors, mostly Black women—found this path of taking atrocity and turning it into voice and agency.

...........................................................

**ALSO THESE IRISH-FACED** women from Charlestown who told me it was possible to bring this stuff back to a neighborhood like mine, where everybody also had Irish faces.

...........................................................

**THAT BECAME A** gift. The deaths of my siblings, the tragedies of my family—those things weren't killing me anymore.

...........................................................

***EASTER RISING*** is a book that pretends to be about getting out, but it's really about getting back.

...........................................................

**THERE WAS A** party line to stick to. Part of that was being controlled by organized crime. Part of it was being seen as a bastion of white supremacy that needed to be broken, without the understanding that many of us in Southie were already broken.

...........................................................

**"WEIRD" WAS A** word that was used a lot. If you had an idea. Or if you thought a particular kind of candy was cool. "What are you, fuckin' weird?"

...........................................................

**PUNK ROCK WAS** a kind of deprogramming for me—exposure to things that would be considered "weird."

...........................................................

**PEOPLE WOULD GO** wandering and find each other. That happened at the Rathskeller. It happened at underground parties on Thayer Street.

...........................................................

**THAYER STREET IS** now one of the fanciest art streets in Boston. People have no idea what it was like. Such a dingy, wild street.

...........................................................

**ON ST. PATRICK'S** Day, you search Instagram and the Southie parade is all people with green shamrock stickers on their faces—and they're tech bros!

...........................................................

**SOME OF THE** fanciest restaurants now were once bloodbath taverns.

...........................................................

**PEOPLE FROM** working-class and poor communities are used to their stories being told by the courts, police and newspapers. I work with different groups to help them transform trauma into voice and agency and to use their story.

...........................................................

**PEOPLE THINK IT'S** about, How did you get out? And it is partly about getting out, but only because I found a way to embrace all I come from.

# PHYLLIS ELLISON-FEASTER

*RETIRED TEACHER*

**FOR ME, IT** wasn't about desegregation. It was about my right to attend South Boston High School. As a Black student, I had the same right as white students.

**WE MOVED FROM** Mattapan to Roxbury in '74. Matter of fact, we got the notice about South Boston High when we moved there. My mom didn't realize that was the high school my brother and I would attend.

**WE GOT ON** the bus that morning and went to Bayside Mall to pick up students from Harbor Point. Going towards South Boston High, we saw waves and waves of people protesting.

**THAT'S WHEN I** thought, *Wow, this is something big.* Because, like I said, we'd just moved there. We didn't know.

**YOU SEE THESE** white people out with babies in carriages, shouting.

**CAMERAS IN FRONT** of the school. People shouting at the buses. Frightening.

**I WAS 14** at that time.

**WE HAD TO** go through metal detectors because it was so hostile inside the building. State troopers inside the building, particularly that first year.

**I THINK BUSING** was well-intentioned. I don't think it met the objective.

**WHAT WAS THE** real purpose? Black students were on one side of the classroom. White students on the other.

**I WENT BACK** to South Boston High to do my student teaching. I wanted to show the Black students there that you can achieve. You can go to college.

**I COULD NEVER** have walked down G Street or D Street to the store when I was a student. Now Black people live there and it's not a big deal.

# SUHAYL RAMIREZ

*WINE PROFESSIONAL*

**I AM FROM BOSTON.** There are so few of us left! I was born in New York and moved here when I was 6. My entire family is from the Dominican Republic. Boston is 1,000 percent home.

**ROXBURY FEELS LIKE** home in this really amazing way. I am quite literally in the center of Nubian Square.

**IT WAS AMAZING** to be here in the midst of our protest summer. Watching waves and waves of people in front of my doorstep. Joining them at certain times. And really feeling like, my gosh, everything I've ever known about Roxbury is true. This community is so amazing and resilient.

**PEOPLE FORGET, BECAUSE** there's always so much emphasis on what's not working.

**THERE'S STILL VERY** much a formality to wine. Like, we're talking about wine and that's all that matters. Terroir. Climate. OK, cool, let's talk about climate change and how it affects the people who pick the grapes. Who picks the grapes?

**I HOSTED AT** Toro after they first opened. I learned wine doesn't have to be pretentious. We're having tapas, put it in a tumbler—just a big party.

**YOU KNOW WHAT'S** kept me here? Opportunity. It's easier to connect, easier to navigate, easier to meet people. I kind of like the smallish pond here.

**URBAN GRAPE IS** a small-footprint wine shop in the South End, but it has national reach and attention.

**THERE AREN'T** enough of us who are ready to admit that a small pond is OK.

**AND THAT IT'S** OK to want to be a slightly bigger fish.

**IT'S A LITTLE** big city. Do I wish things stayed open till 4 a.m.? Absolutely.

# MATT TAYLOR

*TRACKSMITH FOUNDER*

**UNLIKE OTHER CITIES,** you can meet someone who grew up in Boston who never ran a step in their life, but they can tell you about a moment in the Boston Marathon. They remember.

**THE EASY ANSWER** is that Tracksmith is a running apparel brand based in Boston. The longer answer is much more about the ethos and culture of running.

**RUNNING IS AN** individual sport. Maybe we're in the same club or we're teammates, but I'm not passing you a ball. But if you and I both run the Boston Marathon, that's a shared experience that bonds us.

**THE SHARED EXPERIENCE** of pushing yourself as hard and as fast as you can. There's so much power in the shared suffering.

**WHEN WE WERE** starting the brand, I just looked at all my running clothes. They didn't link at all to the way I dressed to go about the rest of my life.

**IT'S VERY MUCH** driven by a New England sensibility. That understated approach to things.

**WE JUST PUT** our heads down and go to work. Reserved. Quiet.

**WE TAKE OUR** time. We think two or three or four steps ahead. We're not super reactive and always, "What's the latest trend? What do we have to do to this?" We have a plan. We're executing against the plan.

**IN NEW YORK,** you're always trying to climb to the top. That creates amazing energy, and when I go to New York, I love it. The energy in Boston is different. It's quieter and steady in a way I find appealing.

**THE CHARLES IS** just such an iconic place to run. There will literally be hundreds of people out there in the course of the day.

**PUT A PIN** anywhere in New England and you're within two or three hours of coast, mountains, lakes, everything.

STORIES

_Essays and selected writing from
noted Boston voices_

# FENWAY CONFESSION

*Written by* **SAM GRAHAM-FELSEN** | **ONE COOL, DRIZZLY DAY** in 1998, I found myself walking through an unmarked side door into the bowels of Fenway Park, reporting for my first day of work. I'd finally made it to the Show.

From the time I was a kindergartener growing up in Jamaica Plain I'd been obsessed with the Red Sox, dreaming of one day working at Fenway. I was too young to remember the brutal 1986 World Series loss. I was barely conscious of the Curse of the Bambino. All I knew was that my hometown team had the greatest pitcher in the world, Roger Clemens; the greatest hitter in the world, Wade Boggs; and an up-and-coming star named Mike Greenwell, with cool flip-down shades and baseball's greatest nickname: the Gator. Going to Fenway with my dad—watching these gods grace that pristine field— was the highlight of my young years.

I also remember watching, with unbelievable envy, the sunburnt peanut vendors stalking the aisles, tossing snacks to fans. *How the hell did those guys get that job?* It seemed like the single greatest gig imaginable. Not only did you get to watch the Sox for free, you got to be vicariously famous. You were part of the show—a Fenway peanut guy! People from all across the country and around the world took pictures of you. You got *paid* to be a tourist attraction.

Becoming a vendor seemed as unlikely as getting drafted into the Major Leagues. But it turned out, in classic Boston fashion, that you simply had to know a guy. My guy was a buddy from high school, Eric, who would eventually land at least two dozen of my friends and relatives vendor jobs. That first day, I followed Eric to a dank, cavernous room underneath the right field stands. An avocado-shaped woman [I'll call her Gracey] with big gold reading glasses draped around her neck sat on a platform behind a huge U of a desk. A throng of a hundred or so vendors huddled around her, half of them beanpole teens and college kids, half of them paunchy, aging malcontents who worked day jobs as UPS guys or landscapers or the like. Gracey was the only female in the room. She looked down at us like a frowning queen, raised her glasses and began to read names off a sheet.

"Raw-bits," she called out.

"Dogs, home," replied Roberts, one of the older guys.

I quickly understood that Gracey called names in order of seniority. The longer and more consistently you worked at Fenway, I soon learned, the higher you climbed in the vendor hierarchy. The very top guys all chose to sell hot dogs in the home plate section, where the richest fans sat. [This was before beer was sold in the stands, when Puritanical "blue laws" still dominated Boston.] The least desirable item, in 1998, was Diet Coke. The least desirable section was the bleachers, cheap seats behind the outfield. I was the last-ranked guy in the room, so that's what I got: Diet Coke, bleachers.

I vividly remember walking out into the bleachers for the first time, in that cool spring drizzle, carrying a tray of 24 soda bottles on my head. The tray was gridded, and it dug into my skull. [I would soon learn to pad the inside of my cap with a wad of napkins.] I walked up what felt like a thousand steps, all the way to the nosebleeds in the very back row, calling out, "Diet Coke. Diet Coke heeeeere!"

I didn't make a single sale. I got laughed at. One drunk guy called out, in circa-1998-Boston-meathead fashion, "Diet Gay!"

By the end of the first inning, I was soaking wet. My head and neck throbbed with pain. I took a breather near the exit ramp, and a veteran vendor passed by me. He looked at my full tray of sodas and shook his head.

"Dude," he said. "You haven't sold a single one yet?"

I shook my head in shame.

"You gotta *sell* it. You gotta yell, kid! Like this. 'Hey, everybody, this kid's got DIET COKE. DIEEEEEE-IT COKE HEEEAH, DIE-IT COKE! WHO NEEDS ONE? DIET COKE HEEEAH!' Like that. Gawt it? *Scream*."

So I took a deep breath, turned around to face the fans and hollered, "HEY, DIEEEEEE-IT COKE HERE!" as I walked all the way up another set of stairs. Still, nothing.

Then it hit me—my problem. It was "here." I was saying it all wrong. I seemed to be the only vendor in the entire park *pronouncing* the *r*.

Contrary to Hollywood myth, plenty of Bostonians don't have a Boston accent. Who does has a little to do with class and ethnicity, more to do with who raised you. Virtually all the working-class Irish and Italians I grew up with—the Bostonians whom Hollywood loves to make movies about—had the accent. But I also knew plenty of upper-middle-class Irish and Italian kids, as well as WASPs and Jews and Black people, who obliterated their *r*'s. What they had in common is that their parents were from Boston. If your parents hailed from elsewhere, you almost certainly didn't have the accent. My parents came from [whisper it] New York.

Now I realized that without a Boston brogue, I would never be taken seriously as an "authentic" Fenway vendor.

"Eyyyy, Diet COKE heah," I belted. "GETcha Diet Coke heah-hhhhhhh!"

It was a chilly, rainy day. I was hawking a cold, comically expensive diet beverage in the bleachers, where no one gave a damn about their caloric intake. I still faced long odds. But I kept screaming, with ever-greater Boston-accented fervor, and eventually, a guy raised his hand, and I passed a bottle down his row, and he passed me a five, and when I started to pass him back his change, he told me, "Keep it."

I sold only two or three more sodas that day, but I left the park exhilarated. The more I acted like a caricature—a screaming, badass Bostonian lunatic—the more product I sold. And little by little, I worked my way up Gracey's rankings. Halfway through the season, I was no longer relegated to the dreaded Diet Coke slot. I was selling popcorn, ice cream bars, Cracker Jacks. By my second year at Fenway, I was even selling regular Coke. And while I never made it all the way up to hot dogs, by my third or fourth year, I was selling peanuts, the second-most-prestigious product in the park. Once I'd made it to peanuts, my confidence skyrocketed, at least inside Fenway.

In real life, I was a timid nerd, terrified of confrontation. I went to the top high school in the city, Boston Latin; followed all the rules; ran away from fights; and barely engaged in underage drinking, fearing an arrest record would mess up my college applications. But once I entered Fenway, I became a grisly Boston bro. When people told me to get out of their way, I'd snap back, "Cool it, pal. I'm workin'!" When customers complained about exorbitant prices, I'd bark, "Take it ah leave it!" Watching seasoned vendors, I learned to intimidate fans into

giving me a tip, staring them down as I slowly jingled the quarters in my apron. In the rare instances that I didn't get the wave, I'd say, extra loud, "*Oh, my bad* ... I didn't realize ya wanted ya QUAWTAHS back." And then, as I passed down the quarters, invariably some other fan in the aisle would turn to me, say, "What a cheap *prick*," and not only buy a bag of peanuts but proudly tell me to keep the change. I was constantly rewarded for terrible manners. I had one of my best days ever when I imitated one of the top-ranked vendors and shouted, over and over again, "Grabbbbbbb ya NUTS!"

[That day, I made over 300 bucks in commission and tips for about two hours of work. That was another irony of the job. We were seen as working-class grunts, sweating for quarters, but veteran vendors could make professional-consultant wages, at least per hour.]

On rare occasions, someone complained. One of us would throw a bag of peanuts. The fan would fail to catch it. It would end up hitting a kid or senior citizen in the head. The vendor would walk off without apologizing. We would then get a fake-stern talking-to from the higher-ups about how we vendors were the faces of "Friendly Fenway," we needed to get our acts together, etc. And then we'd go back out the next day and be just as rude and rowdy.

The truth was, ballpark management was perfectly happy with our behavior. This is what Boston was famous for: salt-of-the-earth jerks, people who flip you the bird for the most innocuous traffic blunders, turf warriors who tell you to get the "fahk" off their "prawpitty" when you're just walking down the street. *Friendly Fenway? Gimme a fahkin' break.*

Of course, this was just the stereotype based on half-truths—one I happily helped perpetuate, even as the real Boston was straying further and further from that myth. I didn't know all of this at the time, but the stereotype is largely based on the Boston of the 1970s. That Boston was, in the words of historian Rick Perlstein, "America's most tribal city." It got that way because, for generations, Boston's "ethnic whites"—mostly Irish and Italian—had been discriminated against by the city's Protestant elites, the so-called Boston Brahmins. Little by little, the ethnic whites accumulated power, which they were loath to share. They became fiercely territorial: The Irish stayed in Southie and Charlestown, the Italians stayed in the North End and Eastie, and everyone made sure Black Bostonians stayed in Roxbury and the

South End. The tension came to a head in 1974, when Boston began integrating public schools. Many of the city's ethnic whites revolted, refusing to send their kids to school and stoning buses carrying Black children. One group of teenagers from Southie and Charlestown attacked a Black man with an American flag, in broad daylight, in the middle of City Hall Plaza, right in front of a news photographer. The photo made the front page of the *Boston Herald American*, won the Pulitzer Prize and has sullied Boston's image ever since.

**AN IRONY OF THE JOB: WE WERE SEEN AS WORKING-CLASS GRUNTS, SWEATING FOR QUARTERS, BUT VETERAN VENDORS COULD MAKE PROFESSIONAL-CONSULTANT WAGES, AT LEAST PER HOUR.**

Again, I didn't really know any of this at the time. I was born in 1981. By that point, most of the racial violence had died down. When I was growing up, I definitely sensed that Boston had a chip on its collective shoulder, but I chalked most of this up to the hideously cold winters and the Curse of the Bambino. The Red Sox hadn't won a World Series since 1918, while our hated rival, the Yankees, had won about a billion. Of course Bostonians were a little cranky.

But by the time I was working at Fenway, Boston had less to whine about. It was becoming a biotech hub, brimming with millionaire yuppies and fine-dining establishments. Gleaming new tunnels and grassy public squares replaced the rusting overpasses of "Dirty Old Boston." The famously stingy Red Sox—who sold Babe Ruth, the Bambino of lore, for pennies—had new owners willing to shell out for top talent. We had acquired one of the greatest pitchers of all time, Pedro Martinez, and two of the greatest hitters of all time, Manny Ramirez and David Ortiz. All three were Dominicans, and incidentally, Dominicans had become one of the largest minority groups in Boston. Little by little, the city shed its status as one of America's whitest cities. Today, the majority of Bostonians are non-white, unthinkable in the '70s.

In 2004, my last season, the Red Sox pulled off the most dramatic comeback in baseball playoff history against the Yankees, then crushed the Cardinals in the World Series. I was there—technically selling peanuts, but really just watching the games in utter disbelief. Since then, the Red Sox have won three more World Series. The Celtics and Bruins have also won championships in the ensuing years, and of course, don't even get me started on the Patriots, who have brought an obscene number of trophies home to my once-victory-starved city.

The chip on the shoulder, if it still exists, is a prop, part of an act. Most old Bostonians are happy. Their dingy triple-deckers are selling for seven figures, allowing them to buy mansions in Florida and escape the brutal Boston winters. And new Bostonians? They're friendly. Don't be surprised when you walk down the street and hear a kind stranger ask, with no Boston accent whatsoever, "How *are* you?"

But if you're coming to Boston to hear the accents—if you want to be told, by a screaming, stubbly goon, to grab your nuts—you can still head to Fenway.

**SAM GRAHAM-FELSEN** is the author of *Green*, a novel about growing up in Boston. His prized possession is a ball Pedro Martinez tossed him during pre-game warm-ups in 2001.

# STREETS AND STORIES

*Written by* **DART ADAMS**

**COUNTLESS TIMES,** I've fallen into heated debates, with both born-and-bred Bostonians and longtime residents alike. What neighborhood is a house, school or business in? Is it in Chinatown? Is it in the Theater District? The Leather District? Where does Roxbury stop being called Roxbury and instead become Longwood Medical and Academic Area? I've spent many man-hours explaining moving borders and looking at street parking signs for clarification. I'm usually vindicated. Several times I have been humbled. Damn you, Bay Village! Just a word of advice: If you want to avoid a heated Boston debate, do not ask locals if Donna Summer is from Roxbury or Dorchester. Alternatively, if you enjoy chaos? Do it.

Boston streets—especially the ones in my neighborhood, which is Lower Roxbury and/or the South End, depending on where you stand—just don't follow any traditional grid format. They don't align with north, east, west and south. Instead they tend to run northeast, southeast, northwest, and southwest. Our borders are just as unruly. Neighborhoods bleed into one another. Side streets run alongside main streets, and boundaries blur. You can often think you're in one Boston neighborhood, but you're actually in another. You can overshoot an entire neighborhood just by walking five minutes down a major thoroughfare.

For example, Massachusetts Avenue runs for 16 miles through several towns. I grew up near the corner that marked the South End/Lower Roxbury border. Going toward and past Boston City Hospital along Mass. Ave. took you into Lower Roxbury. So did going down Tremont Street, past the Piano Craft Guild Apartments—known to locals as The Piano Factory—toward Ruggles Street station.

No signs tell you you're no longer in the South End, unless you look at individual parking signs along Tremont and Columbus, which inform you that you're now in Roxbury.

South End connects to Lower Roxbury on one side and the Back Bay on another. By chance, I recently found the marker denoting the border of the South End and Back Bay. It's almost hidden on a wall across the street from the Orange Line's Mass. Ave. station, on the side of a structure tucked between the station exit and an assisted-living community. Most people will never see the green-and-white sign that says, "END OF SOUTH END. WELCOME TO BACK BAY." They won't know that the station itself is in one neighborhood, but the Subway right next door is in another.

This is barely the tip of the iceberg.

Follow Columbus Ave. from Egleston Square at the border of Jamaica Plain and Roxbury into Roxbury to Roxbury Crossing station, you'll be at 1234 Columbus Ave. Even the bus stop on the corner says, "COLUMBUS AVENUE." However, at the next crosswalk we reach Malcolm X Boulevard. Cross the street on the same side and you'll arrive at the Reggie Lewis Center, which bears the address of 1350 Tremont Street. Pardon me? Where did Columbus Ave. go? Not to fret. Walk past Ruggles Street station on the opposite side of the street and you'll discover Columbus has now jumped one street over, running parallel to Tremont.

This is how the city of Boston does its magic tricks with geography—tricks the natives learn to live with and use to their advantage.

Growing up in the South End and Lower Roxbury, I never really wanted a car. I was close to everywhere I wanted to go already. [Plus, there never seemed to be anyplace to park.] Also, my neighborhood contains hundreds of public alleys—narrow and often almost hidden—that as kids we referred to as Warp Zones. We'd used this seemingly endless maze of back streets, side streets and public alleys to either get into mischief or escape it. Today, they don't show up on Google Maps.

Once you hit Dartmouth Street, there's the Back Bay station across the way from Copley Place Mall, which is connected to the Prudential Center by a skywalk and leads to Boylston Street, which runs parallel to Newbury Street.

If you take another side street or two, you'll eventually reach Commonwealth Ave. and the Commonwealth Avenue Mall, leading to the Public Garden and Boston Common. Pro tip: You can reach the

Charles River quick from Boylston if you turn onto Newbury then take a right on Fairfield, then follow Fairfield Street until it brings you to the bridge that takes you across a highway to the beautiful Charles River Reservation.

I could go on. The streetscape is a puzzle, but there are many solutions. It's all just a matter of knowing where you are.

\*\*\*

South End, Lower Roxbury and Back Bay make an extremely aesthetically pleasing stretch of Boston. There are numerous brownstones, cul-de-sacs and rotaries with small parks with fountains in the middle, such as Braddock Park, Rutland Square and Union Park along Columbus and Tremont. Trees and gardens line many streets.

It's classic Boston in so many ways, and yet the true history of the communities that live and have lived in this pocket of the city is a story of Boston that almost never gets told, especially not in the mass media.

Boston is, famously, a city obsessed with its own place in history. However, the full richness of Roxbury and South End, one of the city's most vibrant, diverse and historically significant neighborhoods, goes almost unmarked and uncommemorated. With the passage of time, the neighborhood has gone through changes and transitions. Some things are vastly improved and more convenient. But the history of the neighborhood can become obscured by new development and the displacement of people who lived here generations ago.

I grew up along the 400 block of Mass. Ave. between 1975 and 1999. At one point the Boston chapter of the NAACP had its office at 451 Mass. Ave., directly across the street from the Harriet Tubman House at 566 Columbus Ave., a community center recently demolished, revealing a vista of brownstone backstairs. Ella Little-Collins, Malcolm X's older sister, used to live in an apartment across from my building at 487 Mass. Ave. These sites were key to the history of the community and civil rights in Boston but are now unmarked.

Quieter forms of history also unfolded here. At each end of that block, there was a rivalry between New York House of Pizza—formerly Ugi's Subs—and South End House Of Pizza, now known as South End Pizza & Grill. Neighborhood residents were often torn on which spot to visit. Half of my family would order from one, and the other half the other—frustrating to me, since I'd have to go pick up both orders. There were neighborhood stores where they knew you by name and knew your families because they'd been there for a generation or more. Brown's Market, Morales Market, Kosmos Market and Braddock Drug, which was at George's Barber Shop at 777 Tremont, now occupied by A-1 Barber Shop. My barbershop is now Cut

**THERE'S A STORY HERE THAT DOESN'T FIT THE STEREOTYPICAL NARRATIVE OF BOSTON BRAHMINS AND IRISH IMMIGRANTS.**

N Edge, at 410 Mass. Ave., formerly home to Skippy White's record store in the '80s and early '90s—a shop known for soul and R&B, and the only store that specialized in rap records and tapes locally until about 1986.

Back when the South End/Lower Roxbury was a jazz mecca between the early '30s and early '60s, that same spot was home to the Savoy Café, favorite hangout of Malcolm X and Nat Hentoff, the great jazz critic and free-speech advocate. Martin Luther King Jr. lived right across the street when he attended Boston University in pursuit of his doctorate. He met New England Conservatory of Music student Coretta Scott in this same neighborhood. Sammy Davis Jr. grew up in the South End/Lower Roxbury, too. He lived in multiple rooming houses along Columbus Ave. as a member of the Will Mastin Trio with his father Sammy Davis Sr. and his "uncle" Will Mastin, including at Mother's Lunch at 510 Columbus Ave.

Sadly enough, no plaques highlight these landmarks of historical and cultural significance. There's a story of diversity and creative culture here that doesn't fit the stereotypical narrative of Boston Brahmins and Irish immigrants.

As a kid, we visited the neighborhood playgrounds, sure to get home before the streetlights came on. There was Carter Playground, Titus Sparrow Park, O'Day Playground, Peters Park, Ringgold Park and Derby Park. Around 1981, Teddy Bear Arcade opened up at the corner of Stuart and Church, right before the Theater District. It drew gamers from all over—kids from the nearby Josiah Quincy

School, Don Bosco High, Boston High and Blackstone School, as well as college students from Northeastern University, Emerson College and Boston University. Kids from Chinatown, the South End, Lower Roxbury and the Back Bay all converged at one of the few places where young people of all backgrounds could be part of a community not related to sports. Even local gangs deemed it a neutral site.

Along Tremont Street between the late '70s and the late '90s, there were apartments populated mostly by Latino residents, predominantly Puerto Ricans. On the sunny side of the street, starting from the library, there was Kosmos Market on the corner. Then Ida's Bridal Shop, which made cakes so amazing people special-ordered them for birthday parties. There was a neighborhood church and a company that specialized in moving people to and from Boston and Puerto Rico. And on the corner at the end of the block was Casa Cuong, the quintessential corner store that everyone visited.

Salsa, merengue and dancehall reggae poured out of storefronts, and freestyle and Latin hip-hop, R&B and rap played from neighborhood windows, passing cars' stereo systems and out of Walkman headphones. Down to the corner of West Dedham, the housing complex called Villa Victoria came to be after years of the activist organization IBA [Inquilinos Boricuas en Acción] clashing with the Boston Redevelopment Authority over housing for the growing Latino population. By 1976, over 400 units of affordable housing were built, spread among several complexes. The only spots still remaining from this bygone era are the neighborhood Chinese takeout place Yum Mee Garden and Casa Cuong, still hanging in there at the end of block, albeit directly across the street from a Starbucks.

The neighborhood was once home to landmark establishments like the Hi-Hat, Estelle's and Bob the Chef's. The latter has been replaced by the Southern restaurant Darryl's Corner, but Slade's Bar & Grill and Charlie's Sandwich Shoppe are still where they've been since the South End/Lower Roxbury was a prime destination for Harlem jazz musicians arriving by train at the nearby Back Bay Station. Wally's Cafe Jazz Club was located directly across the street before it moved to the location it has occupied since 1979: the lone jazz venue still in operation from the neighborhood's glory days. Students from the New England Conservatory of Music, Boston Conservatory at Berklee and Berklee College of Music still perform there and continue to busk along Mass. Ave., Boylston and Newbury in the spring and summer months. The sounds evoke memories of generations past, when the neighborhood was alive with lounges and clubs on every block and corner.

My neighborhood was also the home of Allan Rohan Crite, an American master painter who created the first depictions of Black life in Boston, now shown in museums and galleries nationwide. Mel King, an activist, politician, poet and historian, wrote the history of the neighborhood, *Chain of Change*. He also created and oversaw the South End Technology Center on Columbus Ave. shared by both the Methunion Manor Cooperative and nearby Tent City Apartments, housing developments created by community leaders and South End/Lower Roxbury residents who fought for affordable and equitable housing in their neighborhood in 1967 and 1968.

The area has gone through a great deal of changes over the past 20 years. There are skyscrapers and high-rises where none previously existed. Luxury apartment complexes and new developments spring up where there'd previously been nothing for years. Many of the working-class folks and families who once inhabited the South End and Lower Roxbury have been priced out by steadily climbing rents. But regardless of the turnover, my neighborhood still manages to retain its identity as a crossroads of diversity, creativity and culture. It's forever Black and Latino at its core.

---

**DART ADAMS** is a journalist, historian/fact checker, lecturer and author from Boston. He's written for *Complex*, NPR, *Mass Appeal*, Okayplayer, *Ebony*, *Boston Globe Magazine*, *Boston Magazine* and hosts two podcasts, *Dart Against Humanity* and *The Boston Legends Podcast*.

*Poetry by* **FRANKIE CONCEPCION**

## TIDAL

A breeze steals my breath,
and on a current of wind
carries it to our destination before us.

Hours later, on a wave, sand
swallows my feet before
I can take another step.

The tide, rising, catches us
complacent on a shoal,
and in the sudden

tension between movement
of limb and weight of water,
slips salty love letters unto our skin.

Ashore, you tell me how some sharks
make homes of movement, live
on the feel of current between teeth

and my own skin grows
sandpaper-thick. Before we know it
we are standing, once again,

knee-deep in the warm hands of
silt and seaweed, a tide-pool
of jewel-colored fish falling like

offerings at our feet. What a love: to find us
where we stand, if only to remind us
that we have always been made of fullness.

# SEDIMENTARY

sand-filled, sun-baked shoe
forgotten

    child's pink pail, half a castle
    pressed inside

        pair of earrings placed for safekeeping
        into frayed pocket

            wad of gum pulled
            from lover's mouth and chewed, before spitting


arrowhead,
harm undone by Time

    who, as in an hourglass, buries
    the jutting ribcage of a hollow home in shifting sand

            bleached bones: a seagull caught in a net
                and plastic and plastic and plastic

                    an avalanche of shoreline
                    molasses-thick

and a 20-ries coin, oil-slick-
        coaxed from a drowning pocket
                tossed for luck
                    thrown into a bargain

specks of sand kicked into
        oysters' mouths in the hopes that
                they might one day
                    be considered precious

## PATRIOTIC BODY

And what do you know of belonging?
You who were once fed by many mouths.
Who pledged allegiance to the dream
before ever seeing the dreamer, and along
their footsteps, drew your borders.
Flag-hued, loyal mirror of the sky.
Future mother of thieves. Forget
that you ever had another name, or children
around whom you closed your island like a fist.

*One day*, you say, *I will birth*
*the people who would steal that*
*city on a hill and they will call it Beacon.*

---

**FRANKIE CONCEPCION** is a writer from the Philippines and the founder of the
Boston Immigrant Writers Salon. She has been nominated for a Pushcart Prize, was
named Sibling Rivalry Press' 2019 Undocupoet Fellow, and has been part of the
editorial teams of *GLRSQUASH* and *Winter Tangerine*. Her work has been published
in *Joyland*, *HYPHEN*, *Bodega* and *Rappler*, amongst others.

# HARVARD COLLEGE

*Written by* **HENRY ADAMS**

From *The Education of Henry Adams, Chapter IV* [1918]

**THE NEXT REGULAR STEP** was Harvard College. He was more than glad to go. For generation after generation, Adamses and Brookses and Boylstons and Gorhams had gone to Harvard College, and although none of them, as far as known, had ever done any good there, or thought himself the better for it, custom, social ties, convenience, and, above all, economy, kept each generation in the track. Any other education would have required a serious effort, but no one took Harvard College seriously. All went there because their friends went there, and the College was their ideal of social self-respect.

Harvard College, as far as it educated at all, was a mild and liberal school, which sent young men into the world with all they needed to make respectable citizens, and something of what they wanted to make useful ones. Leaders of men it never tried to make. Its ideals were altogether different. The Unitarian clergy had given to the College a character of moderation, balance, judgment, restraint, what the French called *mesure*; excellent traits, which the College attained with singular success, so that its graduates could commonly be recognized by the stamp, but such a type of character rarely lent itself to autobiography. In effect, the school created a type but not a will. Four years of Harvard College, if successful, resulted in an autobiographical blank, a mind on which only a water-mark had been stamped.

The stamp, as such things went, was a good one. The chief wonder of education is that it does not ruin everybody concerned in it, teachers and taught. Sometimes in after life, Adams debated whether in fact it had not ruined him and most of his companions, but, disappointment apart, Harvard College was probably less hurtful than any other university then in existence. It taught little, and that little ill, but it left the mind open, free from bias, ignorant of facts, but docile. The graduate had few strong prejudices. He knew little, but his mind remained supple, ready to receive knowledge.

What caused the boy most disappointment was the little he got from his mates. Speaking exactly, he got less than nothing, a result common enough in education. Yet the College Catalogue for the years 1854 to 1861 shows a list of names rather distinguished in their time. Alexander Agassiz and Phillips Brooks led it; H. H. Richardson and O. W. Holmes helped to close it. As a rule the most promising of all die early, and never get their names into a Dictionary of Contemporaries, which seems to be the only popular standard of success. Many died in the war. Adams knew them all, more or less; he felt as much regard, and quite as much respect for them then, as he did after they won great names and were objects of a vastly wider respect; but, as help towards education, he got nothing whatever from them or they from him until long after they had left college. Possibly the fault was his, but one would like to know how many others shared it.

The Class of 1858, to which Henry Adams belonged, was a typical collection of young New Englanders, quietly penetrating and aggressively commonplace; free from meannesses, jealousies, intrigues, enthusiasms, and passions; not exceptionally quick; not consciously skeptical; singularly indifferent to display, artifice, florid expression, but not hostile to it when it amused them; distrustful of themselves, but little disposed to trust any one else; with not much humor of their own, but full of readiness to enjoy the humor of others; negative to a degree that in the long run became positive and triumphant. Not harsh in manners or judgment, rather liberal and open-minded, they were still as a body the most formidable critics one would care to meet, in a long life exposed to criticism. They never flattered, seldom praised; free from vanity, they were not intolerant of it; but they were objectiveness itself; their attitude was a law of nature; their judgment beyond appeal, not an act either of intellect or emotion or of will, but a sort of gravitation.

This was Harvard College incarnate, but even for Harvard College, the Class of 1858 was somewhat extreme. Of unity this band of nearly one hundred young men had no keen sense, but they had equally little energy of repulsion. They were pleasant to live with, and above the average of students—German, French, English, or what not—but chiefly because each individual appeared satisfied to stand alone. It seemed a sign of force; yet to stand alone is quite natural when one has no passions; still easier when one has no pains.

Into this unusually dissolvent medium, chance insisted on enlarging Henry Adams's education by tossing a trio of Virginians as little fitted for it as Sioux Indians to a treadmill. By some further affinity, these three outsiders fell into relation with the Bostonians among whom Adams as a schoolboy belonged, and in the end with Adams himself, although they and he knew well how thin an edge of friendship separated them in 1856 from mortal enmity. One of the Virginians was the son of Colonel Robert E. Lee, of the Second United States Cavalry; the two others, who seemed instinctively to form a staff for Lee, were town-Virginians from Petersburg. A fourth outsider came from Cincinnati and was half Kentuckian, N. L. Anderson, Longworth on the mother's side. For the first time Adams's education brought him in contact with new types and taught him their values. He saw the New England type measure itself with another, and he was part of the process.

Lee, known through life as "Roony," was a Virginian of the 18th century, much as Henry Adams was a Bostonian of the same age. Roony Lee had changed little from the type of his grandfather, Light Horse Harry. Tall, largely built, handsome, genial, with liberal Virginian openness towards all he liked, he had also the Virginian habit of command and took leadership as his natural habit. No one cared to contest it. None of the New Englanders wanted command. For a year, at least, Lee was the most popular and prominent young man in his class, but then seemed slowly to drop into the background. The habit of command was not enough, and the Virginian had little else.

The lesson in education was vital to these young men, who, within ten years, killed each other by scores in the act of testing their college conclusions. Strictly, the Southerner had no mind; he had temperament. He was not a scholar; he had no intellectual training; he could not analyze an idea, and he could not even conceive of admitting two; but in life one could get along very well without ideas, if one had only the social instinct. Dozens of eminent statesmen were men of Lee's type, and maintained themselves well enough in the legislature, but college was a sharper test. The Virginian was weak in vice itself, though the Bostonian was hardly a master of crime. The habits of neither were good; both were apt to drink hard and to live low lives; but the Bostonian suffered less than the Virginian. Commonly the Bostonian could take some care of himself even in his worst stages, while the Virginian became quarrelsome and dangerous. When a Virginian had brooded a few days over an imaginary grief and substantial whiskey, none of his Northern friends could be sure that he might not be waiting, round the corner, with a knife or pistol, to revenge insult by the dry light of *delirium tremens*; and when things reached this condition, Lee had to exhaust his authority over his own staff. Lee was a gentleman of the old school, and, as every one knows, gentlemen of the old school drank almost as much as gentlemen of the new school; but this was not his trouble. He was sober even in the excessive violence of political feeling in those years; he kept his temper and his friends under control.

Adams liked the Virginians. No one was more obnoxious to them, by name and prejudice; yet their friendship was unbroken and even warm. At a moment when the immediate future posed no problem in education so vital as the relative energy and endurance of North and South, this momentary contact with Southern character was a sort of education for its own sake; but this was not all. No doubt the self-esteem of the Yankee, which tended naturally to self-distrust, was flattered by gaining the slow conviction that the Southerner, with his slave-owning limitations, was as little fit to succeed in the struggle of modern life as though he were still a maker of stone axes, living in caves, and hunting the *bos primigenius*, and that every quality in which he was strong, made him weaker; but Adams had begun to fear that even in this respect one 18th-century type might not differ deeply from another. Roony Lee had changed little from the Virginian of a century before; but Adams was himself a good deal nearer the type of his great-grandfather than to that of a railway superintendent. He was little more fit than the Virginians to deal with a future America which showed no fancy for the past. Already Northern society betrayed a preference for economists over diplomats or soldiers—one might even call it a jealousy—against which two 18th-century types had little chance to live, and which they had in common to fear.

\*\*\*

If the student got little from his mates, he got little more from his masters. The four years passed at college were, for his purposes, wasted. Harvard College was a good school, but at bottom what the boy disliked most was any school at all. He did not want to be one in a hundred—one per cent of an education. He regarded himself as the only person for whom his education had value, and he wanted the whole of it. He got barely half of an average. Long afterwards, when the devious path of life led him back to teach in his turn what no student naturally cared or needed to know, he diverted some dreary hours of faculty-meetings by looking up his record in the class-lists, and found himself graded precisely in the middle. In the one branch he most needed—mathematics—barring the few first scholars, failure was so nearly universal that no attempt at grading could have had value, and whether he stood 40th or 90th must have been an accident or the personal favor of the professor. Here his education failed lamentably. At best he could never have been a mathematician; at worst he would never have cared to be one; but he needed to read mathematics, like any other universal language, and he never reached the alphabet.

**THE VIRGINIAN WAS WEAK, THE BOSTONIAN HARDLY A MASTER OF CRIME. BOTH WERE APT TO DRINK HARD AND TO LIVE LOW LIVES.**

Beyond two or three Greek plays, the student got nothing from the ancient languages. Beyond some incoherent theories of free-trade and protection, he got little from Political Economy. He could not afterwards remember to have heard the name of Karl Marx mentioned, or the title of *Capital*. He was equally ignorant of Auguste Comte. These were the two writers of his time who most influenced its thought. The bit of practical teaching he afterwards reviewed with most curiosity was the course in Chemistry, which taught him a number of theories that befogged his mind for a lifetime.

Harvard College was a negative force, and negative forces have value. Slowly it weakened the violent political bias of childhood, not by putting interests in its place, but by mental habits which had no bias at all. It would also have weakened the literary bias, if Adams had been capable of finding other amusement, but the climate kept him steady to desultory and useless reading, till he had run through libraries of volumes which he forgot even to their title-pages. Rather by instinct than by guidance, he turned to writing, and his professors or tutors occasionally gave his English composition a hesitating approval; but in that branch, as in all the rest, even when he made a long struggle for recognition, he never convinced his teachers that his abilities, at their best, warranted placing him on the rank-list, among the first third of his class. Instructors generally reach a fairly accurate gauge of their scholars' powers. Henry Adams himself held the opinion that his instructors were very nearly right, and when he became a professor in his turn, and made mortifying mistakes in ranking his scholars, he still obstinately insisted that on the whole, he was not far wrong. Student or professor, he accepted the negative standard because it was the standard of the school.

He never knew what other students thought of it, or what they thought they gained from it; nor would their opinion have much affected his. From the first, he wanted to be done with it, and stood watching vaguely for a path and a direction. The world outside seemed large, but the paths that led into it were not many and lay mostly through Boston, where he did not want to go.

\*\*\*

In his opinion the education was not serious, but in truth hardly any Boston student took it seriously, and none of them seemed sure that President Walker himself, or President Felton after him, took it more seriously than the students. For them all, the college offered chiefly advantages vulgarly called social, rather than mental.

Unluckily for this particular boy, social advantages were his only capital in life. Of money he had not much, of mind not more, but he could be quite certain that, barring his own faults, his social position would never be questioned. What he needed was a career in which social position had value. Never in his life would he have to explain who he was; never would he have need of acquaintance to strengthen his social standing; but he needed greatly someone to show him how to use the acquaintance he cared to make. He made no acquaintance in college which proved to have the smallest use in after life. All his Boston friends he knew before, or would have known in any case, and contact of Bostonian with Bostonian was the last education these young men needed. Cordial and intimate as their college relations were, they all flew off in different directions the moment they took their degrees. Harvard College remained a tie, indeed, but a tie little stronger than Beacon Street and not so strong as State Street. Strangers might perhaps gain something from the college if they were hard pressed for social connections.

Socially or intellectually, the college was for him negative and in some ways mischievous. The most tolerant man of the world could not see good in the lower habits of the students, but the vices were less harmful than the virtues. The habit of drinking—though the mere recollection of it made him doubt his own veracity, so fantastic it seemed in later life—may have done no great or permanent harm; but the habit of looking at life as a social relation—an affair of society— did no good. It cultivated a weakness which needed no cultivation. If it had helped to make men of the world, or give the manners and instincts of any profession—such as temper, patience, courtesy, or a faculty of profiting by the social defects of opponents—it would have been education better worth having than mathematics or languages; but so far as it helped to make anything, it helped only to make the college standard permanent through life. The Bostonian educated at Harvard College remained a collegian, if he stuck only to what the college gave him. If parents went on generation after generation, sending their children to Harvard College for the sake of its social advantages, they perpetuated an inferior social type, quite as ill-fitted as the Oxford type for success in the next generation.

The Harvard graduate was neither American nor European, nor even wholly Yankee; his admirers were few, and his critics many; perhaps his worst weakness was his self-criticism and self-consciousness; but his ambitions, social or intellectual, were necessarily cheap even though they might be negative. Afraid of such serious risks, and still more afraid of personal ridicule, he seldom made a great failure of life, and nearly always led a life more or less worth living. So Henry Adams, well aware that he could not succeed as a scholar, and finding his social position beyond improvement or need of effort, betook himself to the single ambition which otherwise would scarcely have seemed a true outcome of the college, though it was the last remnant of the old Unitarian supremacy. He took to the pen. He wrote.

*\*\*\**

What Henry Adams said in his Class Oration of 1858 he soon forgot to the last word, nor had it the least value for education; but he naturally remembered what was said of it. He remembered especially one of his eminent uncles or relations remarking that, as the work of so young a man, the oration was singularly wanting in enthusiasm. The young man—always in search of education—asked himself whether, setting rhetoric aside, this absence of enthusiasm was a defect or a merit, since, in either case, it was all that Harvard College taught, and all that the hundred young men, whom he was trying to represent, expressed. Another comment threw more light on the effect of the college education. One of the elderly gentlemen noticed the orator's "perfect self-possession." Self-possession indeed! If Harvard College gave nothing else, it gave calm. For four years each student had been obliged to figure daily before dozens of young men who knew each other to the last fibre. One had done little but read papers to Societies, or act comedy in the Hasty Pudding, not to speak of regular exercises, and no audience in future life would ever be so intimately and terribly intelligent as these. Self-possession was the strongest part of Harvard College, which certainly taught men to stand alone.

Whether this was, or was not, education, Henry Adams never knew. He was ready to stand up before any audience in America or Europe, with nerves rather steadier for the excitement, but whether he should ever have anything to say, remained to be proved. As yet he knew nothing. Education had not begun.

---

**HENRY ADAMS**—descendent of John and John Quincy Adams—was born on Beacon Hill's Mount Vernon Place in 1838. His histories and novels of American life in the early- and mid-19th century stand as literary classics. *The Education of Henry Adams,* published only privately during his lifetime, won the Pulitzer Prize in 1919. [This selection has been abridged.]

INDEX

# INDEX

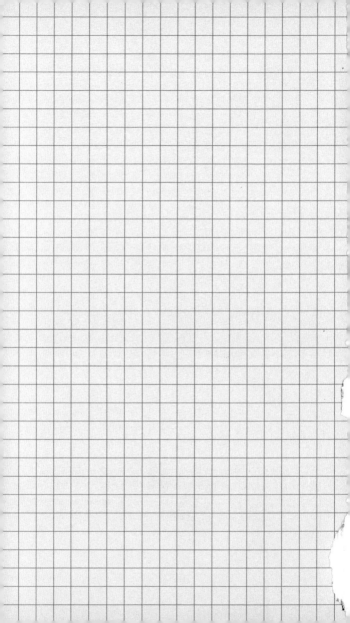